Getting Started with BN4L and GTT Integrations for SAP

Freight Collaboration with SAP Business Network for Logistics and Global Track and Trace

Prince Tyagi
Anevershika

Apress®

Getting Started with BN4L and GTT Integrations for SAP: Freight Collaboration with SAP Business Network for Logistics and Global Track and Trace

Prince Tyagi
Texas, TX, USA

Anevershika
Noida, Uttar Pradesh, India

ISBN-13 (pbk): 979-8-8688-1404-4
https://doi.org/10.1007/979-8-8688-1405-1

ISBN-13 (electronic): 979-8-8688-1405-1

Managing Director, Apress Media LLC: Welmoed Spahr
Acquisitions Editor: James Robinson-Prior, Divya Modi
Editorial Assistant: Gryffin Winkler

Cover designed by eStudioCalamar

Cover image designed by Andreas from Pixabay

Distributed to the book trade worldwide by Springer Science+Business Media New York, 1 New York Plaza, New York, NY 10004. Phone 1-800-SPRINGER, fax (201) 348-4505, e-mail orders-ny@springer-sbm.com, or visit www.springeronline.com. Apress Media, LLC is a Delaware LLC and the sole member (owner) is Springer Science + Business Media Finance Inc (SSBM Finance Inc). SSBM Finance Inc is a **Delaware** corporation.

For information on translations, please e-mail booktranslations@springernature.com; for reprint, paperback, or audio rights, please e-mail bookpermissions@springernature.com.

Apress titles may be purchased in bulk for academic, corporate, or promotional use. eBook versions and licenses are also available for most titles. For more information, reference our Print and eBook Bulk Sales web page at http://www.apress.com/bulk-sales.

Any source code or other supplementary material referenced by the author in this book is available to readers on GitHub. For more detailed information, please visit https://www.apress.com/gp/services/source-code.

If disposing of this product, please recycle the paper

Table of Contents

About the Authors

 **Prince Tyagi** belongs to a farmer family from the village of Kulsath in Uttar Pradesh, India. He is a SAP consultant and a holder of multiple patents in supply chain and sustainability. As a freelance technical writer and reviewer, Prince writes extensively on the topics of enterprise supply chain, asset management, and sustainability and has more than 14 years of experience as a solution specialist in SAP PM, SAP TM, SAP iMRO, SAP CS, and SAP QM modules. He has worked in multiple ECC and SAP S4HANA E2E implementations, rollouts, enhancements, and support and upgrade projects spread across various domains and sectors like retail, FMCG, aviation, manufacturing, healthcare, chemical, defense, and software.

 **Anevershika** completed her Bachelor of Engineering from Oxford College of Engineering in Information Science. She also holds a Postgraduate Diploma in Operations and Supply Chain Management. Anevershika comes with a robust 13-year career in IT, having worked with multinational companies like Birlasoft, IBM, Airtel, and HCL. She

brings over five years of specialized experience as a functional consultant in SAP ERP applications and more than six years as a developer in CRM applications. Her extensive background includes leading multiple end-to-end implementations, rollouts, enhancements, and support and upgrade projects across various domains.

About the Technical Reviewer

 **Rajesh Ojha** is Principal Architect at SAP America and a certified SAP S/4HANA EAM professional. He has over 15 years of SAP consulting experience across a variety of complex projects, roles, and responsibilities, such as, oil and gas, construction, manufacturing, transportation, and chemicals and pharmaceuticals. His areas of expertise are in SAP Asset Management Portfolio, Enterprise Digital Transformation, and providing strategy consulting to business leaders on how to best leverage SAPs potential power in their organization.

Introduction

Overview: Embracing the Future of Supply Chain with SAP BN4L and SAP GTT

In today's fast-paced and interconnected world, supply chains have evolved beyond straightforward, linear processes. They now function as intricate, adaptable systems that must quickly respond to shifting market conditions, rising customer expectations, and unforeseen global events. Conventional logistics and transportation management approaches often lack the speed, visibility, and flexibility required by modern enterprises. To meet these growing demands, SAP offers two robust, cloud-driven solutions—SAP Business Network for Logistics (BN4L) and SAP Global Track and Trace (GTT)—designed to revolutionize supply chain management.

This book serves as a comprehensive, practical resource for understanding and applying these advanced tools. It equips supply chain experts, strategic decision-makers, and technical professionals with the insights and guidance needed to effectively deploy, integrate, and extract maximum value from SAP BN4L and SAP GTT.

What Are SAP BN4L and SAP GTT?

At the heart of this transformation are two interconnected solutions:

> **SAP Business Network for Logistics (SAP BN4L)** is a cloud-based solution designed by SAP to bring together key players in the logistics space—like shippers, transport companies, freight agents, and logistics partners—onto one digital platform. By centralizing collaboration, it streamlines logistics operations and provides real-time insight into

supply chain activities. This helps organizations eliminate inefficiencies caused by disjointed communication methods, manual processes, and a general lack of transparency across transportation workflows.

As supply chains grow more international and multifaceted, relying on outdated communication tools like emails and phone calls no longer meets the demands of modern logistics. SAP BN4L addresses these shortcomings by enabling businesses to collaborate digitally using standardized workflows. It supports features like live event tracking, automated freight tendering, issue resolution, and streamlined billing, all backed by shared, real-time data.

SAP Global Track and Trace (SAP GTT) is another cloud-powered offering from SAP, created to provide end-to-end insight into the status and location of goods as they move through the supply chain. Whether items are in transit, stored in a facility, or already delivered, SAP GTT gathers and interprets real-time data from various touchpoints, helping companies monitor every step of the product journey.

In today's complex supply networks, which often involve numerous vendors, logistics providers, and customers across different regions, having real-time visibility is crucial. SAP GTT fills this gap by acting as a centralized event management system that gives companies the tools to react quickly to delays or disruptions, enhancing both control and efficiency throughout the supply chain.

Key Objectives of SAP GTT

The primary goal of SAP GTT is to enable **real-time, transparent, and event-driven monitoring** of business processes and logistics flows. With SAP GTT, businesses can

- Track the status and location of goods at every stage of the supply chain

- Predict delays and deviations from the planned schedule

- Automatically trigger alerts and exception workflows

- Ensure compliance with service-level agreements (SLAs)

- Enhance customer service with accurate estimated time of arrival (ETA) predictions

- Integrate with IoT devices and third-party systems for rich contextual data

SAP GTT is not limited to transportation tracking. It can also be used in **production monitoring, order tracking, return logistics, asset tracking, and more**, making it a powerful tool for broader supply chain event intelligence.

Together, SAP BN4L and SAP GTT offer a powerful combination of **real-time visibility, collaboration, automation, and intelligence**, allowing companies to operate more efficiently, improve service levels, and respond rapidly to unexpected changes in supply chain conditions.

Why This Book Matters

The logistics and transportation industry is at a turning point. With rising fuel costs, regulatory complexities, customer expectations for faster deliveries, and constant pressure to reduce environmental impact, companies are re-evaluating how they manage their end-to-end logistics operations.

INTRODUCTION

This book serves as both a **technical reference** and a **business guide**. It introduces key concepts and architecture behind SAP BN4L and SAP GTT and then dives into use cases, integration scenarios, best practices, and configuration details. By the end, readers will understand not only how these systems work but also **how to use them strategically** to unlock value and competitive advantage.

What You Will Learn

Here's a snapshot of what readers can expect to gain:

- A complete overview of SAP BN4L and SAP GTT functionalities

- Step-by-step walkthroughs of common logistics processes like freight order tendering, confirmation, and event tracking

- Practical guidance on integrating with SAP Transportation Management (TM) and SAP S/4HANA

- Insights into key interfaces, APIs, and message flows for electronic data exchange

- How to manage master data (e.g., locations, carriers) both manually and via replication

- Strategies for handling dispute resolution, invoicing, and exceptions within the network

- Real-world examples and case studies of successful implementations

- Best practices for deployment, configuration, and scaling in enterprise environments

The Digital Transformation Journey

SAP BN4L and SAP GTT are not just tools—they are enablers of digital transformation. Organizations that embrace these platforms are setting themselves up for a smarter, more resilient future. Digital supply chains powered by SAP technologies are capable of self-adjusting, self-monitoring, and self-optimizing through automation and real-time insights. For instance:

- Freight tenders can be initiated, accepted, and confirmed automatically based on rules, capacity, and real-time status.

- Exceptions such as shipment delays or missing documentation can trigger alerts and corrective workflows before issues impact the customer.

- Stakeholders across the network—suppliers, carriers, and customers—can collaborate transparently using a shared, cloud-based infrastructure.

This represents a **paradigm shift** away from manual spreadsheets, fragmented email communication, and siloed systems toward a digitally connected, intelligent logistics ecosystem.

Who This Book Is For

This book is designed to serve a wide audience:

- **Business leaders** seeking to understand the strategic value of SAP BN4L and SAP GTT

- **Project managers and consultants** implementing SAP logistics solutions

- **SAP TM and S/4HANA users** integrating with the SAP BN4L

- **IT professionals and developers** working with APIs, interfaces, and master data synchronization

- **Logistics and supply chain professionals** aiming to improve operational visibility and control

Whether you are beginning your journey or seeking to expand existing capabilities, this book provides the foundation and advanced insights you need to succeed.

A Future-Ready Supply Chain

SAP BN4L and SAP GTT prepare organizations for the future—one in which logistics networks are dynamic, responsive, and intelligent. As supply chains continue to face disruption from geopolitical shifts, climate change, and technological evolution, **adaptability and visibility** will become even more critical.

By adopting these SAP solutions, companies not only solve today's problems—they build a foundation for **long-term resilience and agility**. From predictive shipment delays to collaborative transportation planning, these platforms give businesses the tools to thrive in the next generation of logistics.

Final Thoughts

This book is more than a manual—it's a road map for organizations looking to lead in the era of intelligent supply chains. As you move through the chapters, you'll gain both technical knowledge and strategic clarity about how to implement and optimize SAP BN4L and SAP GTT.

The future of logistics is **connected, transparent, and data-driven**— and with the guidance in this book, you're ready to step into that future with confidence.

In the modern supply chain, companies face a multitude of challenges, including global trade complexities, evolving customer expectations, disruptions due to unforeseen events, and the need for compliance with increasingly stringent regulatory requirements. This book addresses these challenges and illustrates how SAP BN4L and SAP GTT can help organizations tackle them. With **SAP BN4L**, businesses can optimize collaboration with suppliers, carriers, and logistics providers, ensuring that every stakeholder in the supply chain is aligned and informed. By integrating digital tools to enhance visibility, SAP GTT helps companies track the progress of goods, predict potential delays, and act proactively to mitigate risks, improving overall efficiency and responsiveness.

While the book explains the technical aspects of SAP BN4L and SAP GTT, it also emphasizes their practical applications in real-world business scenarios. By integrating these solutions, organizations can automate and optimize key logistics processes, such as order fulfillment, inventory management, freight planning, and transportation execution. The book offers practical case studies and examples to demonstrate how companies have successfully adopted these SAP solutions to reduce operational costs, improve delivery accuracy, and enhance customer satisfaction.

A central theme in the book is the idea of digital transformation. As the supply chain landscape evolves, businesses must adapt to new technologies and processes. The book shows how adopting SAP BN4L and SAP GTT can drive this transformation, enabling organizations to build intelligent, connected supply chains.

Whether you are new to SAP systems or an experienced user looking to refine your expertise, this book is designed to cater to a broad audience. Beginners will find clear, easy-to-follow explanations of the fundamental concepts behind SAP BN4L and SAP GTT, while experienced users can delve deeper into more advanced topics, such as system configuration, integration, and best practices for maximizing the value of these tools. The book guides readers through the complexities of logistics management in the digital age, making it an invaluable resource for anyone involved in supply chain, logistics, IT, or operations management.

SAP BN4L

SAP Business Network for Logistics (SAP BN4L) is a robust, cloud-enabled platform created to unify all parties involved in the logistics value chain. By providing a single, connected environment, it facilitates smoother collaboration between businesses and key logistics partners—including shippers, carriers, freight forwarders, and suppliers. Through this integrated network, companies can achieve full operational visibility, improve process efficiency, and harness real-time insights to refine their logistics strategies.

This section explores the core functionalities, strategic advantages, and practical use cases of SAP BN4L, emphasizing its role in transforming supply chain operations.

1. **Overview of SAP BN4L**

   As part of SAP's larger mission to digitize and connect enterprise operations, SAP BN4L is built on the SAP Business Technology Platform (BTP). It equips businesses with advanced tools to manage transportation, logistics, and supply chain processes through a centralized system. By linking companies directly to a wide range of logistics providers, the platform ensures real-time communication, seamless system integration, and data transparency. These capabilities help businesses minimize delays, control costs, and increase their responsiveness to market demands.

2. **Standout Features of SAP BN4L**

   SAP BN4L offers a wide array of features that support every stage of the logistics process:

- **Integrated Ecosystem Collaboration**: The platform supports easy integration with both SAP and non-SAP systems, making it possible for companies to exchange data fluidly with external logistics partners. This leads to better coordination, real-time tracking of deliveries, and more effective management of logistics KPIs.

- **Real-Time Supply Chain Monitoring**: One of BN4L's most valued features is its ability to provide instant updates on shipment movements, inventory availability, and order progress. This allows organizations to identify and resolve issues quickly, improving service reliability.

- **Smart Automation Capabilities**: Leveraging AI and machine learning, the platform automates repetitive logistics tasks such as determining optimal routes, predicting demand, and balancing stock levels. This reduces reliance on manual input and cuts down on errors.

- **Advanced Data Analytics**: The system collects extensive operational data, which is then analyzed to generate insights for improving logistics performance. Businesses can use these insights to refine decision-making and drive continuous improvement.

- **Complete Transparency Across the Chain**: SAP BN4L provides a window into every step of the logistics process. Whether a product is in transit, in storage, or delayed, businesses have up-to-date information at their fingertips, allowing for better coordination and accountability.

- **Support for Compliance and Sustainability Goals**: The platform includes tools to monitor environmental impact and ensure compliance with global standards and regulations. Businesses can track emissions, adjust practices to reduce their carbon footprint, and align with regulatory frameworks such as ISO or GDPR.

3. **Advantages of Using SAP BN4L**

   Organizations that implement SAP BN4L stand to gain several operational and strategic benefits:

   - **Boosted Operational Efficiency**: Automating workflows and enabling real-time updates help businesses cut down on errors, reduce waiting times, and improve resource utilization.

   - **Lower Costs**: SAP BN4L contributes to cost savings by optimizing delivery routes, reducing storage expenses, and minimizing wasted mileage or idle stock. Improved partner collaboration also helps lower contract and transportation overheads.

   - **Enhanced Customer Satisfaction**: With accurate, real-time shipment tracking and faster problem resolution, businesses can deliver a more transparent and reliable service to their customers—fostering trust and loyalty.

   - **Stronger Supply Chain Collaboration**: By promoting open data exchange and synchronized planning with partners, SAP BN4L helps prevent bottlenecks, improves responsiveness, and enables proactive resolution of issues.

- **Scalability for Growth**: The platform is built to grow with the business. As logistics operations expand—across regions or with new partners—BN4L adapts without compromising performance or visibility.

- **Eco-friendly Operations**: Through more efficient routing, better warehouse usage, and emissions tracking, SAP BN4L supports environmentally responsible logistics practices, helping companies meet their green targets.

4. **Use Cases of SAP BN4L**

SAP BN4L can be leveraged across multiple domains and industries. Key applications include

- **Transportation Optimization**: Businesses can manage route planning, carrier engagement, and freight expenses more effectively, leading to faster and more economical delivery operations.

- **Inventory and Warehouse Control**: By connecting with warehouse systems, SAP BN4L ensures real-time stock data is always available. This helps reduce surplus inventory and maintain lean operations.

- **Demand Forecasting**: Using historical data and predictive algorithms, businesses can better anticipate market needs, avoiding both overstock and shortages and aligning supply with demand more precisely.

- **Supplier Relationship Management**: The platform supports better coordination with suppliers by enabling shared data access, real-time order tracking, and performance monitoring—all of which strengthen supplier partnerships.

- **Risk Mitigation**: Real-time operational insight allows businesses to detect and address potential issues—like shipment delays or compliance risks—before they escalate into costly disruptions.

5. **Implementation Considerations and Potential Hurdles**

   Despite the many advantages, adopting SAP BN4L is not without challenges:

   - **Integration Complexity**: For companies using outdated or fragmented systems, connecting to SAP BN4L can require significant effort, planning, and investment in data integration.

   - **Data Quality Requirements**: The effectiveness of the platform is highly dependent on the accuracy and consistency of input data. Poor data can reduce visibility and hinder automation.

   - **Partner Alignment**: The success of the platform also depends on external partners' willingness and ability to participate. Without buy-in from carriers and suppliers, the flow of real-time information can be disrupted, reducing the platform's effectiveness.

CHAPTER 1

SAP BN4L Primer

SAP BN4L is a comprehensive platform designed to facilitate seamless collaboration across the logistics value chain. It leverages cloud-based technology to connect businesses with their partners, such as shippers, freight forwarders, carriers, and suppliers, creating a unified ecosystem. This network offers end-to-end visibility, operational efficiency, and data-driven insights, enabling businesses to streamline their logistics and supply chain operations.

In this chapter, we'll review some of the basics, such as supply chain challenges, business, and partnerships, which will lay the foundation for the remainder of the book when we delve into the core features, benefits, and potential applications of SAP BN4L, alongside its role in enhancing supply chain efficiency.

A Closer Look

SAP BN4L is part of SAP's broader strategy to digitize business operations across various industries. It is built on the SAP Business Technology Platform (BTP), providing a suite of tools for businesses to optimize their logistics, transportation, and supply chain functions. The platform connects businesses with their logistics ecosystem, integrating systems and enabling real-time data sharing, tracking, and collaboration. Through SAP BN4L, organizations can tap into a global network of logistics service providers to improve transparency, reduce costs, and enhance overall operational agility.

© Prince Tyagi, Anevershika 2025
P. Tyagi and Anevershika, *Getting Started with BN4L and GTT Integrations for SAP*,
https://doi.org/10.1007/979-8-8688-1405-1_1

It plays a pivotal role in enhancing supply chain efficiency by fostering collaboration among business partners through a robust network. This platform facilitates the joint management of transactions, seamless exchange of documents, and sharing of insights across the value chain. Such capabilities empower business users to capture, process, and store essential tracking information about their operations. Additionally, it provides the ability to query specific business processes and access comprehensive, end-to-end data visibility.

One of the standout features of this network is its ability to connect shippers with carriers, streamlining collaboration. For instance, shippers can invite carriers to join the network, enabling efficient cooperation in areas such as freight tendering, subcontracting, milestone reporting, freight settlement, and dock appointment scheduling. By bridging communication gaps, this system ensures greater transparency and operational harmony across the supply chain.

The SAP BN4L Freight Collaboration and SAP GTT solution offers a comprehensive, cloud-based platform that includes a variety of solution-owner apps tailored to facilitate daily business operations. These applications are designed to optimize workflows, track activities, and provide real-time updates, making it easier to manage supply chain logistics effectively.

SAP BN4L revolutionizes the way businesses interact within the supply chain. By offering tools that enhance collaboration, improve process transparency, and simplify tracking, this platform serves as a cornerstone for modern, efficient, and connected logistics management.

Challenges of Supply Chain

As supply chain intricacies escalate, the potential for products to be misplaced, misdirected, pilfered, counterfeited, or simply delayed increases correspondingly. These disruptions and inefficiencies not only incur significant temporal and financial costs but also impede businesses' capacity to sustain a nimble supply chain capable of meeting consumers' escalating demands for convenient and near-instantaneous access to safer, fresher goods and services.

To navigate these challenges, companies must achieve comprehensive end-to-end visibility across their extended supply chain networks. The optimal solution lies in a digital, interconnected supply chain that provides an integrated view of real-time data spanning business partners, systems, and processes, thereby enabling the proactive identification of issues and the facilitation of critical decision-making.

In this chapter, we will explore the key challenges faced by supply chains and discuss how **SAP solutions** help organizations overcome these obstacles to create more agile, efficient, and transparent supply chain operations.

One of the primary challenges in managing a supply chain is maintaining **visibility** across the entire network. As goods move through various stages of production, warehousing, transportation, and final delivery, it becomes difficult to track shipments in real time, particularly in complex, multitier supply chains. Lack of visibility can lead to delayed shipments, missed deadlines, and poor customer satisfaction.

Impact:

- Difficulty in managing inventory
- Inability to respond to disruptions in a timely manner
- Increased risk of stockouts or overstocking
- Poor decision-making due to inaccurate data

Demand Fluctuations and Forecasting Errors

Demand fluctuations are common in supply chains, driven by factors such as seasonality, economic shifts, or unexpected events. Forecasting demand is critical for effective planning, but inaccurate demand predictions can lead to stock imbalances. Overestimating demand may result in excess inventory, tying up capital and storage space, while underestimating demand may lead to shortages and lost sales.

Impact:

- Overstocking or stockouts

- Poor inventory management

- Inefficiencies in production and distribution

Supplier and Vendor Management

Supplier management is a significant challenge in supply chains, particularly when dealing with multiple suppliers across different regions. Ensuring that suppliers meet quality, delivery, and cost expectations can be difficult, especially when there is a lack of clear communication and data exchange. Supply chain disruptions caused by supplier issues, such as delayed deliveries or quality problems, can affect the overall supply chain performance.

Impact:

- Delays in production and delivery

- Increased lead times

- Poor product quality

- Difficulty in managing supplier relationships

Inventory Management

Effective **inventory management** is essential for balancing supply and demand. However, managing inventory across multiple locations and ensuring that products are in the right place at the right time is complex. Poor inventory management leads to unnecessary stock levels, higher storage costs, or missed sales opportunities due to insufficient stock.

Impact:

- Increased carrying costs

- Stockouts or overstock situations

- Increased operational complexity

- Negative impact on customer service

Logistics and Transportation Management

Logistics and transportation are integral parts of the supply chain, but managing a network of transportation providers, route optimization, and tracking shipments in real time can be challenging. Factors like rising fuel costs, changing regulations, and unforeseen disruptions like weather events or traffic jams complicate transportation management.

Impact:

- Increased transportation costs

- Delivery delays

- Inefficiencies in route planning

- Lack of real-time tracking and visibility

Compliance and Regulatory Issues

Supply chains must navigate an ever-growing landscape of compliance and regulatory requirements across different countries and industries. This includes customs clearance, product certifications, and environmental regulations. Failure to comply with these requirements can lead to fines, delays, and reputational damage.

Impact:

- Delays due to customs and regulatory issues

- Increased costs associated with compliance

- Risk of penalties and fines

- Complex paperwork and documentation management

5

Risk Management and Disruption

Supply chains are increasingly vulnerable to disruptions from natural disasters, geopolitical instability, pandemics, and other unforeseen events. Identifying and managing these risks proactively is essential, but many companies still rely on traditional, reactive approaches to risk management, which can be inefficient and ineffective in an increasingly volatile world.

Impact:

- Supply chain delays

- Loss of revenue and market share

- Increased costs to mitigate or recover from disruptions

- Long-term impacts on customer trust and business reputation

SAP Business Technology Platform

SAP Business Technology Platform (SAP BTP) is a comprehensive and versatile solution that empowers businesses to transform and innovate by leveraging advanced technologies and services. It provides a unified environment that integrates data management, analytics, artificial intelligence (AI), application development, and automation to create intelligent and connected enterprises. Let's explore the key aspects and benefits of SAP BTP.

Unified Data Management

SAP BTP offers a robust data management framework that allows businesses to consolidate and manage their data from various sources. This includes structured and unstructured data from on-premises systems, cloud applications, IoT devices, and external data sources. By centralizing data management, SAP BTP ensures data consistency, quality, and security across the organization.

Advanced Analytics

The platform provides powerful analytics capabilities that enable businesses to gain actionable insights from their data. With SAP Analytics Cloud, users can perform advanced data visualization, predictive analytics, and business intelligence. The integration with SAP HANA, a high-performance in-memory database, ensures real-time data processing and analysis, allowing businesses to make informed decisions quickly.

Artificial Intelligence and Machine Learning

SAP BTP incorporates AI and machine learning services that help businesses automate processes, enhance decision-making, and improve customer experiences. The platform offers pre-built AI models and tools for developing custom machine learning algorithms. Businesses can leverage these capabilities to analyze large datasets, identify patterns, and generate predictive insights.

Application Development and Integration

SAP BTP provides a comprehensive suite of tools for developing, deploying, and managing applications. The platform supports various programming languages, frameworks, and environments, including SAP Fiori for user experience design. It also offers APIs and integration services that facilitate seamless connectivity between SAP and non-SAP systems, enabling businesses to create end-to-end workflows and automate processes.

Business Process Automation

With SAP BTP, businesses can automate complex processes and tasks using intelligent workflow management and robotic process automation (RPA). The platform's workflow capabilities allow users to design, execute, and monitor business processes, ensuring efficiency and compliance. RPA tools enable the automation of repetitive tasks, reducing manual effort and increasing productivity.

Extensibility and Customization

SAP BTP's extensibility features enable businesses to tailor the platform to their specific needs. Users can develop custom applications, extensions, and services that integrate with SAP's core solutions. The platform's microservices architecture and cloud-native approach ensure scalability and flexibility, allowing businesses to adapt to changing requirements and market conditions.

Security and Compliance

Security and compliance are integral components of SAP BTP. The platform incorporates advanced security measures, including data encryption, access controls, and threat detection, to protect sensitive information. SAP BTP also ensures compliance with industry standards and regulations, such as GDPR, HIPAA, and SOC 2, providing businesses with the assurance that their data is secure and compliant.

Multicloud and Hybrid Deployment

SAP BTP supports multicloud and hybrid deployment models, giving businesses the flexibility to choose the best deployment strategy for their needs. The platform is available on leading cloud providers, including

AWS, Microsoft Azure, and Google Cloud, as well as SAP's own data centers. This multicloud approach ensures high availability, reliability, and performance.

Collaboration and Innovation

The platform fosters collaboration and innovation by providing a unified environment where business and IT teams can work together. SAP BTP's low-code and no-code development tools enable business users to create applications and automate processes without extensive coding knowledge. This democratization of technology empowers employees to contribute to digital transformation initiatives and drive innovation.

Ecosystem and Partner Network

SAP BTP benefits from a rich ecosystem of partners, developers, and consultants who contribute to the platform's capabilities and offerings. The SAP App Center provides a marketplace for third-party applications and services that extend the functionality of SAP BTP. This vibrant ecosystem ensures that businesses have access to a wide range of solutions and expertise to address their unique challenges.

SAP Cloud Network-Based Collaboration

In the evolving landscape of global business, organizations must work together across a multitude of systems, platforms, and geographical locations. Traditional methods of collaboration, such as relying on email chains, spreadsheets, and manual processes, can be inefficient, error-prone, and slow. To stay competitive, businesses need an integrated, cloud-based platform that can connect partners, suppliers, and stakeholders in real time and enable seamless collaboration across borders. This is where **SAP Cloud Network-Based Collaboration** comes in.

SAP Cloud Network-Based Collaboration refers to the use of SAP's cloud technologies to facilitate real-time, secure, and efficient communication and collaboration between organizations, both internally and with external partners. It leverages cloud-based applications, data sharing, and network connectivity to allow seamless collaboration throughout the supply chain, customer relationships, and product life cycles. By harnessing the power of the SAP BN4L and other SAP solutions, organizations can unlock the full potential of digital collaboration, improving efficiency, reducing costs, and accelerating business processes.

In this chapter, we will explore SAP's cloud network-based collaboration capabilities, how they work, and the advantages they bring to businesses in the modern era. We'll look at how SAP helps organizations connect and collaborate more effectively with their partners, suppliers, and customers, ensuring smoother operations and enhanced business outcomes.

SAP Cloud Network: A Unified Collaboration Platform

SAP's cloud network is a powerful ecosystem that facilitates collaboration between businesses, regardless of their size, industry, or geographic location. Through a variety of applications and services, the SAP Cloud Network provides an integrated platform where organizations can collaborate on key business processes, such as procurement, order management, logistics, and finance.

At the core of SAP's cloud network is the **SAP BN4L**, which connects enterprises with a range of third-party suppliers, service providers, and other business partners. This network provides a unified interface to connect all parties involved, making it easier to exchange information, track transactions, and align business processes. In this context, the term "network-based collaboration" encompasses everything from sharing data and insights to coordinating workflows and managing workflows in real time.

Key Features of SAP Cloud Network-Based Collaboration

SAP's cloud-based collaboration tools are designed to address the needs of organizations that require integrated, efficient, and collaborative approaches to managing their business relationships. These tools bring together a host of functionalities that allow businesses to work together more effectively.

SAP BN4L Integration

The **SAP BN4L** is the foundation of SAP's cloud network-based collaboration. It provides a shared platform where buyers, suppliers, logistics providers, and other third-party service providers can come together to exchange information, track shipments, and share critical documents such as purchase orders and invoices.

- **Global Reach and Connectivity**: SAP BN4L connects organizations across multiple industries and geographies, allowing businesses to work with their existing partners and find new suppliers or customers as needed.

- **Real-Time Information Sharing**: All participants in the network can access updated, real-time information about orders, shipments, inventory, and invoices. This reduces manual updates and communication gaps, ensuring that everyone is on the same page at all times.

- **Automated Transactions**: With SAP BN4L, many transactional processes (e.g., invoicing, procurement, and payments) can be automated, improving speed and accuracy while reducing administrative burden.

SAP Ariba for Procurement Collaboration

SAP Ariba is one of the most widely used solutions within the SAP Cloud Network, designed to streamline procurement and sourcing processes through collaboration. SAP Ariba enables organizations to engage with suppliers in a transparent and collaborative environment.

- **Supplier Collaboration**: Suppliers can submit proposals, respond to RFPs, and track the status of their orders in real time.

- **Contract Management**: Businesses can draft, negotiate, and manage contracts in a digital, cloud-based environment, reducing paperwork and enhancing compliance.

- **Procurement Automation**: By automating procurement processes such as purchase order creation and invoice approval, SAP Ariba helps businesses improve efficiency, reduce errors, and accelerate order-to-pay cycles.

SAP S/4HANA Cloud Integration

SAP's flagship ERP suite, **SAP S/4HANA Cloud**, integrates seamlessly with SAP BN4L, providing businesses with a unified, real-time data platform to manage their internal and external operations. This integration ensures that all parties—both within the organization and across the network—have access to consistent, up-to-date information.

- **End-to-End Process Integration**: SAP S/4HANA Cloud connects procurement, finance, supply chain, and sales teams to ensure that business processes flow smoothly from end to end.

- **Collaborative Workflows**: Teams within and across organizations can collaborate more effectively by sharing data and automating workflows.

- **Data-Driven Decision-Making**: With the real-time data provided by SAP S/4HANA, businesses can make more informed decisions based on accurate insights into inventory, financial transactions, and customer orders.

SAP Fieldglass for External Workforce Collaboration

Managing external workers—whether they are contractors, consultants, or temporary staff—is an important aspect of modern businesses. **SAP Fieldglass**, integrated with SAP BN4L, allows businesses to collaborate effectively with external workforce providers.

- **Vendor Management**: SAP Fieldglass helps businesses manage relationships with contractors, temporary workers, and other service providers.

- **Workforce Collaboration**: External workers can access necessary information, track their hours, and submit invoices, streamlining the relationship between businesses and their external workforce.

- **Compliance and Performance Tracking**: Businesses can monitor the performance of their external workforce and ensure compliance with regulations and contracts.

Benefits of SAP Cloud Network-Based Collaboration

The adoption of cloud network-based collaboration through SAP offers several compelling benefits to businesses.

Enhanced Visibility and Transparency

One of the primary benefits of SAP's cloud network collaboration is the increased **visibility** it offers into all stages of the supply chain, procurement process, and customer interactions. With real-time access to data, businesses can see where their goods are, track order progress, and gain insights into potential bottlenecks or disruptions.

- **Track Shipments**: Businesses can track the status of shipments in real time, monitor inventory levels, and forecast demand.

- **Financial Transparency**: SAP's platform allows for real-time invoicing and payment tracking, reducing delays and improving cash flow management.

- **Performance Monitoring**: Businesses can evaluate the performance of suppliers, vendors, and service providers based on up-to-date metrics.

Improved Efficiency and Speed

Cloud-based collaboration eliminates many of the manual processes that traditionally slow down business operations. Automated workflows, real-time data sharing, and integrated applications help streamline business processes, reducing the time spent on administrative tasks.

- **Automated Processes**: SAP BN4L enables automatic creation of purchase orders, invoices, and payment reconciliation, speeding up the procurement and payment processes.

- **Faster Decision-Making**: Real-time data analysis allows businesses to make faster, data-driven decisions that keep operations running smoothly.

- **Reduction in Errors**: Automating key processes reduces the likelihood of human error, which is common in manual systems.

Cost Savings

By improving collaboration and automating tasks, businesses can reduce operational costs and focus resources on more strategic activities.

- **Reduced Transaction Costs**: With integrated systems, organizations can minimize the time and cost associated with managing paper-based transactions and manual approvals.

- **Fewer Stockouts and Overstocking**: By improving visibility and demand forecasting, businesses can reduce costly stockouts or excess inventory.

- **Optimized Supplier Relationships**: Better collaboration and performance tracking help businesses negotiate better terms with suppliers and improve the overall value of their supply chains.

Scalability and Flexibility

The cloud-based nature of SAP's network collaboration tools means that businesses can easily scale their operations and extend their collaborations with new partners or markets.

- **Rapid Onboarding of New Partners**: With the SAP BN4L, businesses can quickly onboard new suppliers, logistics providers, or customers, without the need for complex integration.

- **Adaptation to Market Changes**: SAP's cloud solutions allow businesses to adapt to market conditions and customer demands quickly, enabling them to stay competitive in a fast-paced environment.

Basic Architecture

The basic architecture of SAP BN4L is designed to facilitate seamless collaboration between shippers and their logistics partners (Figure 1-1). At its core, BN4L leverages the SAP Business Technology Platform (BTP) to provide a secure and integrated environment for managing logistics operations. The platform connects shippers running SAP Transportation Management (TM) with carriers through APIs, web portals, and EDI integration. This setup enables real-time communication, data exchange, and process automation for tasks such as freight tendering, subcontracting, settlement, tracking, and dock appointment scheduling. By centralizing these functions, BN4L enhances visibility, efficiency, and resilience in supply chain management.

At the heart of SAP BN4L is its integration with SAP Transportation Management (TM) and the broader SAP ecosystem. This integration ensures that shippers can seamlessly manage their logistics operations from a single platform. BN4L leverages APIs, web portals, and EDI interfaces to connect with carriers and logistics service providers, facilitating real-time data exchange and communication.

Data management is a critical aspect of SAP BN4L's architecture. The platform consolidates data from various sources, including GPS devices, IoT sensors, ERP systems, and manual inputs. This data is then processed and stored in a secure, centralized repository. SAP BTP ensures data security through advanced encryption, access controls, and compliance with industry standards and regulations.

BN4L offers a user-friendly interface that simplifies the management of logistics operations. The platform provides intuitive dashboards, customizable reports, and interactive maps, allowing users to easily access and interpret data. The user experience is further enhanced by seamless integration with other SAP solutions, such as SAP Fiori, providing a consistent and cohesive experience across the SAP ecosystem.

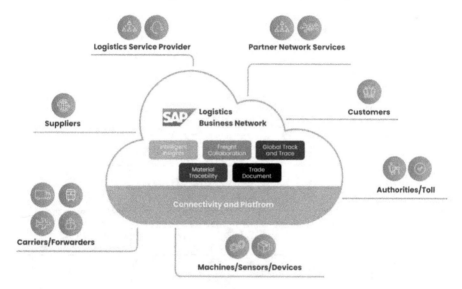

Figure 1-1. *BN4L basic architecture and connectivity*

SAP BN4L Partnerships

SAP has partnered with various companies to support with the implementation of SAP BN4L solutions. **project44** is a leading supply chain visibility platform that connects shippers, carriers, and logistics service providers to deliver real-time tracking and transparency across global transportation networks. It is designed to optimize supply chain operations by providing actionable insights, reducing inefficiencies, and enhancing collaboration among stakeholders. Figure 1-2 shows the integration of the following companies providing services in the fields of carrier collaboration, logistics visibility, and integrity:

- Descartes

- Uber Freight

- Project44

- ShipERP

- Everstream

- PC*Miler

- Scantrust

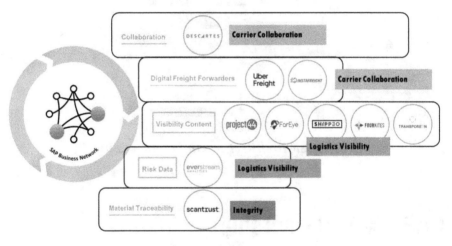

Figure 1-2. *SAP BTP integration with other transportation products*

Summary

Cloud-Based Business Collaboration in SAP marks a significant evolution in how companies operate and engage with external partners. By adopting cloud technology, businesses are now able to simplify and accelerate interactions with customers, vendors, and third-party providers. This shift fosters a more responsive, transparent, and efficient environment for collaboration and innovation.

SAP offers a range of cloud solutions—including SAP Ariba, S/4HANA Cloud, Fieldglass, and Business Network for Logistics (BN4L)—that enable organizations to synchronize operations, digitize manual tasks, and engage with partners across the globe in real time. These tools help streamline communication, boost operational speed, and lower overhead costs, all while increasing the flexibility needed to adapt to rapidly changing business conditions.

As digital transformation reshapes the global marketplace, the ability to collaborate effectively across a distributed network of partners has become essential. SAP's cloud collaboration ecosystem equips companies with the digital infrastructure they need to enhance supply chain coordination, boost productivity, and maintain a competitive edge in a dynamic economic landscape.

SAP's Connected Collaboration Framework provides the infrastructure for linking businesses with external stakeholders across various locations and platforms. With solutions like SAP BN4L, companies can manage logistics workflows in real time—enabling data sharing, transaction processing, and status updates to happen instantly between partners. This results in improved coordination, greater clarity, and faster, more informed decisions.

Overview of SAP BN4L Architecture

At the technical level, SAP BN4L is built to work closely with SAP Transportation Management (TM), acting as a bridge between shippers and their logistics partners. It uses APIs, digital portals, and EDI to facilitate seamless data flow, communication, and automated processes. This architecture supports critical logistics tasks such as carrier selection, freight booking, status tracking, and appointment management at warehouses.

The Role of SAP BN4L in Modern Logistics

SAP BN4L is central to reshaping how companies manage their transportation and supply chain operations. It delivers a unified, real-time platform that boosts collaboration, operational efficiency, and visibility across the entire logistics network. Through deep integration with other SAP systems, organizations gain a consistent, intelligent environment for making smarter, faster decisions and building more resilient logistics strategies.

Looking Ahead

In the next chapter, we'll explore the functional structure of SAP BN4L, focusing on freight collaboration and SAP Global Track and Trace. We'll examine the core components that support comprehensive supply chain monitoring and control, providing a clear picture of how these tools enable end-to-end transparency and strategic agility.

CHAPTER 2

Functional Overview

In today's fast-paced global supply chain, the efficient management of logistics is crucial to staying competitive. Businesses need streamlined, reliable, and transparent processes to move goods from suppliers to customers. This is where SAP BN4L, specifically its Freight Collaboration module, comes into play.

SAP BN4L Freight Collaboration is a cutting-edge, cloud-based solution designed to revolutionize the way organizations collaborate with their logistics partners, including freight carriers, suppliers, and customers. The solution is part of the larger SAP BN4L, which connects businesses with their entire ecosystem to enable end-to-end collaboration.

The Freight Collaboration module in SAP BN4L focuses on optimizing freight transportation, providing a seamless, real-time exchange of information between shippers and carriers. It leverages advanced digital technologies, automation, and integration with SAP's enterprise solutions to create an efficient, transparent, and flexible logistics process.

In this chapter, you will gain an in-depth understanding of SAP BN4L and how it enhances collaboration and efficiency across logistics operations. You will learn about the key features and capabilities of BN4L that enable businesses to streamline their logistics processes and make data-driven decisions.

By the end of this chapter, you will have a clear understanding of how SAP BN4L can transform your logistics operations by enhancing collaboration, providing real-time visibility, optimizing decision-making, and minimizing costs across the supply chain.

© Prince Tyagi, Anevershika 2025
P. Tyagi and Anevershika, *Getting Started with BN4L and GTT Integrations for SAP*,
https://doi.org/10.1007/979-8-8688-1405-1_2

SAP BN4L

SAP Business Network for Logistics (BN4L) is a state-of-the-art, cloud-hosted solution crafted to elevate cooperation across logistics channels and increase overall execution efficiency. It creates a seamless, digital bridge between organizations utilizing SAP Transportation Management (TM) and their carriers or logistics collaborators. This setup allows for the streamlined exchange of data and fosters transparent communication across all stages of the logistics journey.

Through SAP BN4L, enterprises can establish immediate and digitalized relationships with logistics service providers, which not only accelerates task execution but also minimizes the dependency on repetitive manual procedures. The platform is equipped with predefined, collaborative capabilities that simplify the coordination of operations, enable the sharing of vital transport-related files, and promote a consistent flow of essential information throughout the logistics ecosystem. Furthermore, the system adapts to different technological levels among providers by offering diverse connectivity options, which makes it suitable for varied industry contexts. Its architecture ensures easy assimilation into current enterprise infrastructures while leveraging existing transport networks for a smoother flow of operations.

A key strength of the platform lies in its ability to keep a close eye on cargo in motion while documenting critical logistics checkpoints as they happen. It matches anticipated events with what actually occurs, even when data comes from disconnected or diverse systems and partners. This empowers organizations to instantly alert both internal departments and external collaborators when disruptions, delays, or urgent matters arise. Predefined rules can be configured to automatically respond to such situations, ensuring that transportation and logistics flows proceed with minimal disturbance.

BN4L also delivers complete material traceability across the entire supply chain, enabling companies to trace the journey of raw inputs through production and final delivery. This level of clarity supports stronger quality management, enhances accountability, and allows for rapid response during product recalls or similar incidents. A consolidated interface gives a complete overview of all active shipments, while built-in alert tools inside the Logistics Situation Room help identify and resolve issues early. Moreover, BN4L is compatible with third-party risk alert systems via APIs, allowing enterprises to detect and address possible threats before they cause widespread impact.

In addition to real-time management, BN4L offers the tools necessary to evaluate logistics performance and uncover inefficiencies that may be slowing down operations. This analysis aids in refining strategies and boosting performance.

- Freight Collaboration (FC)
- Global Track and Trace (GTT)
- Material traceability
- Intelligent insight

By supporting synchronized operation among different departments and supply chain players, BN4L helps ensure that logistics processes remain tightly integrated and functionally optimized. Decision-makers gain access to live data, enabling them to take swift action when variations from the expected occur. Real-time Freight Collaboration (FC) also plays a pivotal role in removing bottlenecks and fostering unified workflows across organizational boundaries. Utilizing consistent communication models, BN4L cuts down unnecessary expenditures while increasing clarity over goods in transit. With the help of Global Track and Trace (GTT), businesses attain better visibility over inventory movement across their distribution networks, minimizing unforeseen costs. The use of intelligent insight and forward-looking data tools empowers companies to anticipate potential supply chain issues and respond before they affect broader operations.

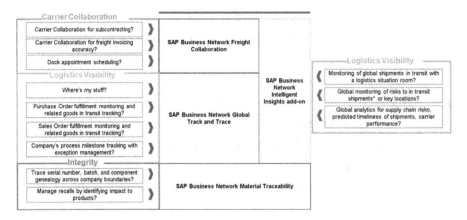

Figure 2-1. *BN4 application*

To achieve seamless logistics execution, it is vital to handle the collaboration between shippers and carriers with precision and clarity. This section provides a detailed examination of the essential workflows that contribute to making these interactions efficient, with a special focus on the capabilities made available through SAP BN4L. By exploring how to deal with freight tendering, contract handling, settlement processes, live tracking, and the coordination of dock appointments, you'll discover practical strategies to reduce operational hold-ups and control logistics expenses.

The upcoming parts offer a closer look at the various ways shippers can initiate quote requests, manage tendering activities, and engage in freight contract discussions effectively. Additionally, real-time shipment monitoring is discussed, highlighting how it plays a crucial role in avoiding unexpected disruptions. You'll also gain insight into how dock appointment scheduling—facilitated through BN4L—can lead to smoother loading and unloading procedures at warehouses and distribution centers.

Beyond individual processes, this section reveals how SAP BN4L acts as a unifying system that brings greater visibility to logistics operations. By using its tools, organizations can foster enhanced coordination with logistics providers, improve the pace and precision of goods movement, and eliminate communication gaps that often lead to inefficiencies. The platform not only supports faster delivery execution but also contributes to long-term reliability in the supply chain by helping maintain strong, cooperative partnerships.

Through a deeper understanding of SAP BN4L's integrated features, logistics professionals can unlock new levels of operational control. This includes greater flexibility in responding to sudden changes, enhanced ability to align transportation planning with real-time updates, and the confidence to make better decisions based on live shipment data. These elements collectively support the goal of elevating performance across logistics activities while ensuring customer demands are consistently met.

Request for Quotation (RFQ)

Shippers can send digital requests for quotations to multiple carriers through the BN4L platform. This allows them to compare prices and services offered by different carriers.

Using the SAP BN4L environment, shippers gain the ability to issue digital quotation requests to several carriers simultaneously. This feature streamlines the process of evaluating various transportation providers by allowing an easy comparison of proposed costs, service levels, and timelines—all within a unified platform.

Tendering

Within SAP BN4L, the **Tendering** feature provides an organized method for initiating transport proposals from carriers. The workflow unfolds in the following steps:

1. **Carrier Response**: After receiving the digital RFQ, carriers submit their pricing models and terms for the requested shipment.

2. **Evaluation and Award**: The shipper reviews and analyzes all the submitted quotes to determine the carrier that aligns best with their cost-efficiency and service needs.

3. **Freight Order**: Upon choosing the most suitable carrier, the system generates a freight order, which is sent out for the carrier's approval.

4. **Subcontracting**: If the selected carrier decides to delegate a portion of the shipment to a third party, BN4L ensures this subcontracting activity is properly recorded and monitored.

Freight Contracting

This part of SAP BN4L is designed for handling end-to-end freight contract life cycles. It supports negotiations, agreement setups, and document exchanges with carriers and third-party logistics providers. Key functionalities include

1. **Freight Order**: Once the carrier is finalized, a detailed freight order—outlining shipment routes, pickup and delivery schedules, and required services—is created and dispatched.

2. **Subcontracting**: If the main carrier chooses to assign part of the job to another carrier, this process is handled transparently within BN4L. The subcontractor, once onboarded, becomes part of the communication loop through the same interface.

Settlement

SAP BN4L simplifies financial reconciliation by providing digital tools to manage billing, payment approvals, and dispute handling. This guarantees that compensation transactions are accurate, auditable, and timely for all entities involved in the logistics process.

Real-Time Transparency

Real-time monitoring is a critical capability in BN4L. It offers **Global Track and Trace (GTT)** of shipment progress, carrier reliability metrics, and prevailing transportation costs. This live data helps shippers make agile decisions, reduce inefficiencies, and achieve greater operational clarity.

Dock Appointment Scheduling

SAP BN4L's **Dock Appointment Scheduling** capability helps manage the timing of vehicle arrivals and departures for loading and unloading, reducing congestion and idle time:

1. **Scheduling**: Shippers arrange appointment windows for carriers, enabling systematic logistics at warehouses and hubs.

2. **API Integration**: Carriers and shippers can communicate in real time via APIs, allowing seamless updates or changes to appointments.

3. **Guest Access**: Carriers not formally connected to the shipper's BN4L network can still schedule appointments using a temporary guest link.

4. **Real-Time Visibility**: The platform displays appointment statuses, making it easier for planners to manage dock activities efficiently.

5. **Gate Management**: Features such as automated check-in/check-out logs further streamline entry and exit procedures at logistics facilities.

SAP BN4L Application Core Functionality for Shippers
Manage Network

- Join the SAP BN4L network cloud platform as a shipper.

- Update and maintain your company profile directly on the platform.

- Send invitations to preferred carriers for onboarding.

- Establish system-to-network connectivity between your SAP instance and BN4L.

- Use search tools to locate and invite matching carriers and logistics providers.

- Simulate and test shipper-carrier setups using test accounts.

- Activate required services and input API credentials to enable digital data flow with external systems.

Dock Appointment Scheduling

- Set up and define which docks can be accessed by specific carriers.

- Manage all scheduled appointments and make updates as needed.

- Restrict appointment visibility to users based on site-specific access control.

- Enable overbooking for high-demand time slots when required.

- View all freight and appointment data associated with a vehicle at the gate.

- Log vehicle arrivals and departures with precise timestamps.

- Group related documents under single or multiple appointment events.

- Log reportable events tied to confirmed bookings.

- Maintain dock, yard, gate, and loading point configurations.

- Allow shared use of docks and gates across entities in similar time zones.

- Permit multi-entity dock sharing with designated partners.

- Block certain dock slots during maintenance or special events.

- Enable appointment booking without time slot selection.

- Adapt schedules dynamically based on live updates.

- Distribute guest URLs for carriers to self-manage appointments.

Manage Location Master Data

- Create, modify, bulk upload, or archive your logistics location data.

Freight Execution

Based on integration readiness, receive detailed freight execution data such as

- Date/time when shipment milestones are reached

- Events tied to container movement, especially in ocean scenarios

- Delay notifications with updated estimated completion times

- Live geo-location pings from vehicles or ships

- Electronic proof of pickup and delivery documents

- Transport methods used, total travel distance, and **carbon emissions** for sustainability tracking

Settlement

Depending on integration, carriers can upload invoice data for freight orders.

- Map SAP-specific charge and condition types to standardized BN4L charge codes.

- Challenge unexpected freight charges submitted by carriers.

- Manage dispute workflows within the platform.

- Collaborate on dispute resolution via BN4L or SAP TM.

- Set dispute thresholds and configure automatic resolution rules.

- Update SAP TM freight order charges once a dispute is closed.

- Restrict visibility of disputes to user-assigned purchase organizations.

- Establish layered approval chains before submitting disputes back to carriers.

Business Operations

- Track all inbound and outbound message exchanges occurring through SAP BN4L.

SAP BN4L Application Core Functionality for Carriers
Manage Network

- Receive invitations to join BN4L from business partners.

- Choose to accept or decline collaboration requests.

- Subscribe to automatic notifications for new invitations.

- Define integration methods for API/EDI connections with external systems.

Freight Order Management

- Confirm, update, or decline freight orders; propose alternate prices if allowed.

- View shipments transmitted from SAP ECC LE-TRA systems.

- Respond to freight quotation requests with updated cost or scheduling options.

- Auto-send quotations upon acceptance or rejection of RFQs.

- Get alerts for any changes to the status of a freight order or quotation.

- Handle ocean booking confirmations and receive shipping documents.

- Process air freight bookings, including validation of IATA and flight code data.

Freight Execution

If the system setup permits, carriers can

- Notify the shipper once scheduled events are completed.

- Alert of any delays with revised expected completion times.

- Send location tracking updates.

- Upload **proof of delivery** and **proof of pickup** documentation.

- Access visibility feeds for event monitoring across ports or terminals.

Settlement

- Create and submit invoices linked to freight orders.

- See freight orders awaiting self-billing by customers.

- Dispute charges tied to unexpected costs or discrepancies.

- Respond to disputes raised by customers.

- Manage billing for both ocean and air freight.

- Issue credit memos to cancel previously submitted invoices.

- Access a history of credit memos raised on your account.

Dock Appointment Scheduling

- Book appointment slots for pickups and drop-offs at warehouses.

- Allow guest carriers to self-manage bookings even without full onboarding.

- Group multiple documents under shared appointment slots.

- Schedule appointments without locking in a time if flexibility is needed.

Business Operations

- Monitor all real-time message exchanges coming in and out of BN4L.

SAP GTT

With the capability to observe and manage the movement of shipments and inventory across the complete supply chain, organizations can significantly enhance the smooth functioning of their logistics processes. This solution delivers an end-to-end, integrated view of logistics events, ensuring that every participant stays informed and aligned with current operations. Such transparency not only minimizes the risk of unanticipated costs but also increases the reliability and responsiveness of the supply chain.

In addition, the SAP BN4L Global Track and Trace offering plays a critical role in raising customer satisfaction by delivering timely and accurate updates regarding order deliveries. Customers gain access to real-time tracking information, which fosters trust and contributes to a more satisfying service experience.

The intelligent insights made available through this platform equip businesses with the power to base their strategies on real-time data. Utilizing live logistics data, companies can fine-tune their operational workflows, remove inefficiencies, and ensure goods are delivered punctually and in the expected condition. Having such visibility and control at hand is essential for sustaining competitiveness in an ever-accelerating market.

In conclusion, the SAP BN4L Global Track and Trace capability serves as a robust solution that enables organizations to proactively address supply chain vulnerabilities, elevate efficiency, enrich customer experience, and make smarter, data-backed decisions through intelligent insights.

SAP Global Track and Trace (GTT)

SAP Global Track and Trace (GTT) is a state-of-the-art solution built to provide comprehensive visibility and traceability across the entire supply chain. It empowers businesses with real-time access to logistics information, allowing them to manage, supervise, and optimize supply chain performance. Below is an outline of the prominent features and advantages of SAP GTT.

Comprehensive Tracking and Monitoring

With SAP GTT, enterprises can observe the movement and condition of shipments at each phase of the logistics chain. From dispatch to final delivery, the system collects data from GPS tracking units, IoT-based sensors, and ERP platforms to offer a unified view of transport statuses.

Event Management

A standout capability of SAP GTT is its ability to handle logistics events in a structured manner. Users can specify critical milestones—such as departures, handovers, and arrivals—and receive automated alerts when these events occur or deviate from expectations. This functionality enables swift action, helping to avoid disruptions and uphold timelines.

Supply Chain Visibility

The solution delivers full-spectrum visibility into logistics activities, starting with suppliers and ending with customers. This clarity helps detect constraints, enhance routing choices, and boost productivity. Real-time awareness allows organizations to react to shifts in supply or demand with agility and precision.

Integration with SAP Solutions

SAP GTT naturally connects with other SAP modules, including SAP S/4HANA, SAP Transportation Management, and SAP Extended Warehouse Management. These integrations ensure seamless information flow, granting users access to consolidated, accurate data for better decision-making across the logistics ecosystem.

Analytics and Reporting

Built-in analytics and reporting tools empower organizations to evaluate their logistics performance using key metrics such as delivery punctuality, carrier effectiveness, and inventory trends. These insights lead to more informed strategies that improve supply chain efficiency and customer service levels.

Exception Management

When unplanned events arise—such as delays, damages, or route changes—SAP GTT's exception management feature detects and flags them. It also recommends suitable resolutions, ensuring that issues are addressed promptly and their impact is minimized.

Collaboration and Communication

The platform encourages seamless collaboration between all participants in the supply chain, including suppliers, logistics providers, and clients. By centralizing communications, SAP GTT improves coordination, reduces misunderstandings, and reinforces mutual trust among stakeholders.

Sustainability and Compliance

In supporting green logistics practices, SAP GTT gives companies the tools to monitor and reduce their environmental impact. It calculates carbon emissions tied to transportation and helps identify areas where sustainability efforts can be improved. Moreover, the solution helps maintain regulatory compliance by offering accurate documentation and timely shipment data.

Scalability and Flexibility

Designed to grow alongside business needs, SAP GTT accommodates industries with various levels of logistical complexity. Whether used for straightforward shipment monitoring or sophisticated multimodal logistics operations, the flexible framework of GTT adapts easily, supporting the expansion of tracking functions as businesses evolve.

Order Fulfillment Monitoring

Continuous Tracking of Goods in Transit

- **Inbound, Outbound, and Intra-company:** SAP GTT supports real-time tracking across all stages of your logistics flow.

    - **Inbound:** Keep a watchful eye on goods coming into your facilities from suppliers.

    - **Outbound:** Follow the progress of deliveries sent from your sites to end customers.

    - **Intra-company:** Track movement of inventory between company warehouses or production sites.

- **Benefits:** Such continuous visibility ensures accurate inventory control, quicker issue resolution, and heightened efficiency across the supply network.

On-the-Fly Key Performance Indicators (KPIs)

- **Determining the Impact of Exceptions:** SAP GTT generates live KPIs that help evaluate the severity and consequences of supply chain deviations. Metrics like actual versus expected transit durations and adherence to promised timelines can be reviewed on the spot.

  - **Real-Time Analysis:** Immediate access to this data lets users quickly spot root causes of problems like route detours or delays.

  - **Proactive Management:** With this level of insight, actions can be taken early to correct errors before they ripple into bigger supply chain disruptions.

Summary

In summary, the SAP BN4L solution provides comprehensive tools for monitoring order fulfillment, ensuring continuous tracking of goods, real-time KPI analysis, and enhanced supply chain transparency, resilience, and sustainability. These capabilities help businesses manage their supply chains more effectively, reduce risks, and improve overall performance

SAP BN4L, specifically its Freight Collaboration module, offers businesses a comprehensive, digital platform to optimize their logistics and freight management. Through real-time tracking, seamless communication, automated payment processes, and data-driven insights, SAP BN4L Freight Collaboration transforms the way companies manage their freight transportation. By fostering better collaboration across the supply chain and providing the tools to make smarter, more informed decisions, this solution enables businesses to drive operational efficiency, reduce costs, and enhance customer satisfaction. In an increasingly competitive global market, SAP BN4L Freight Collaboration is a game-changer for organizations looking to stay ahead of the curve and build more resilient, scalable logistics networks.

SAP Global Track and Trace is more than just a tool for tracking shipments—it's a strategic solution that transforms supply chain management. The solution's real-time visibility, analytics, and proactive risk management capabilities enable businesses to respond to disruptions more quickly, optimize operations, and enhance overall performance. In an increasingly complex global market, having access to accurate, up-to-date information is crucial for staying competitive and meeting customer expectations.

Furthermore, the ability to integrate SAP Global Track and Trace with other SAP solutions, such as SAP Integrated Business Planning (IBP) and SAP S/4HANA, creates a more comprehensive and unified supply chain ecosystem. This integration ensures that data flows seamlessly between systems, enabling better coordination and decision-making across the organization.

The following chapter will provide a comprehensive overview of the tools and maintenance capabilities within SAP GTT and SAP BN4L. We'll explore the key administrative features, monitoring dashboards, configuration tools, and support mechanisms that ensure smooth operation, scalability, and adaptability of these logistics solutions in a dynamic supply chain environment.

CHAPTER 3

Tools and Maintenance

In today's rapidly evolving global marketplace, seamless integration and real-time communication between different systems, partners, and stakeholders are crucial for efficient supply chain operations. SAP BN4L (SAP BN4L) stands at the forefront of this evolution, offering a robust solution for improving logistics collaboration and enhancing supply chain transparency. One of the critical components that enables SAP BN4L to drive these improvements is its Connectivity feature.

The SAP BN4L Connectivity module facilitates seamless integration with various internal and external systems, ensuring that data flows smoothly across the entire logistics network. This connectivity forms the backbone of SAP BN4L, enabling businesses to interact efficiently with their suppliers, customers, freight carriers, and other logistics partners in real time.

In this chapter, we will explore the power of SAP BN4L Connectivity, highlighting its essential role in streamlining communication, improving data exchange, and ensuring that businesses can respond dynamically to changing demands. From the integration with existing ERP systems to the connection with third-party providers, SAP BN4L Connectivity provides a holistic, cloud-based platform that simplifies and automates complex logistics processes.

© Prince Tyagi, Anevershika 2025
P. Tyagi and Anevershika, *Getting Started with BN4L and GTT Integrations for SAP*,
https://doi.org/10.1007/979-8-8688-1405-1_3

SAP BN4L Connectivity not only enables efficient data sharing and process automation but also provides businesses with the flexibility to connect with a wide range of partners across diverse industries and regions. The modular approach of SAP BN4L allows companies to scale their logistics networks as needed, ensuring they can easily adapt to new requirements and expand their operations globally.

By the end of this chapter, readers will have a deeper understanding of how SAP BN4L Connectivity supports businesses in overcoming logistics challenges, optimizing their supply chains, and maintaining competitive advantage in an increasingly interconnected world. Through real-time data exchange, robust system integrations, and seamless connectivity, SAP BN4L Connectivity transforms logistics management into a more agile, collaborative, and efficient process.

In this chapter, you will learn how SAP BN4L enables seamless connectivity and data exchange between shippers, carriers, and SAP systems through a combination of APIs and web portals. The chapter will introduce you to various interfaces and the integration capabilities that streamline logistics operations.

First, we will explore how **API integration** allows carriers to connect their systems to SAP BN4L for efficient electronic data exchange. This integration ensures that critical logistics data, such as shipment details, tracking information, and order updates, are transmitted in real time, reducing manual data entry, minimizing errors, and accelerating decision-making. By leveraging the API network, both carriers and shippers can enhance communication and collaboration, optimizing their logistics processes.

SAP BN4L Connectivity

SAP BN4L connects with SAP and carriers through a combination of APIs and web portals. Here's a brief overview of how it works.

API Integration

Carriers can connect their systems electronically to BN4L via APIs. This allows them to receive and send data with shippers seamlessly. SAP BN4L acts as a "pass-through" network for this data exchange. Carriers can seamlessly connect their systems to SAP BN4L through APIs, enabling efficient electronic data exchange between carriers and shippers. This API integration allows carriers to send and receive critical logistics data—such as shipment details, tracking information, and order updates—directly with shippers in real time. SAP BN4L functions as a "pass-through" network, ensuring that this data flows securely and accurately between all parties, facilitating smoother operations and enhancing collaboration. This streamlined communication eliminates manual data entry, reduces errors, and accelerates decision-making, ultimately optimizing the logistics process for all involved.

Freight Tendering Interfaces

You can perform RFQ-based tendering with SAP BN4L. To do so, you must support sending and receiving messages out of your SAP TM or TM in SAP S/4HANA system. Use the business-to-business (B2B) message interfaces listed in Table 3-1.

Table 3-1. *RFG-based tendering B2B message interfaces*

Interface	Purpose
TransportationOrderQuotation CreateRequest_Out	To send freight requests for quotation to SAP BN4L
TransportationOrderQuotation Confirmation_In	To receive freight quotations from SAP BN4L
TransportationOrderQuotation Notification_Out	To send award notifications to SAP BN4L
TransportationOrderQuotation CancellationRequest_Out	To send cancellations to SAP BN4L

Freight Orders for Confirmation Interfaces

You can perform direct tendering or subcontracting of freight orders with SAP BN4L. To do so, you must support sending and receiving messages out of your SAP TM or TM in SAP S/4HANA system. Use the B2B message interfaces list in Table 3-2.

Table 3-2. *Direct tendering B2B message interfaces*

Interface	Purpose
TransportationOrder Request_Out	To send freight orders for confirmation or direct tendering requests to SAP BN4L
TransportationOrder Confirmation_In	To receive freight order or direct tendering confirmations from SAP BN4L
TransportationOrder CancellationRequest_Out	To send freight order cancellations to SAP BN4L

SAP BN4L provides the capability to directly manage freight tendering processes with external logistics partners through system-integrated communication. This allows transport managers to initiate, confirm, or cancel freight orders digitally without manual follow-ups or delays.

The communication is facilitated by business-to-business (B2B) message interfaces that connect your SAP Transportation Management (TM) or TM in S/4HANA with BN4L. These interfaces use predefined message structures to ensure consistent and automated data exchange.

The following table outlines the required interfaces for direct tendering.

In practice, this means that when a freight planner wants to assign a carrier to a transport order, they can initiate the request from SAP TM. The system then uses the TransportationOrderRequest_Out interface to send this order to BN4L. Once a carrier accepts the order, the confirmation comes back through the TransportationOrderConfirmation_In interface. If the freight order needs to be withdrawn, the TransportationOrderCancellationRequest_Out interface is used.

Confirm Freight Bookings Interfaces

In addition to tendering, SAP BN4L also supports subcontracting freight bookings. This function allows shippers to outsource transport execution by communicating booking details to carriers or service providers. Like direct tendering, this process depends on structured B2B messages exchanged between the SAP system and BN4L.

The messages used here help ensure bookings are confirmed, canceled, or tracked systematically without requiring manual follow-up.

Table 3-3. *Subcontracting of freight bookings interface*

Interface	Purpose
TransportationOrderBooking Request_Out	To create a freight booking request in your SAP BN4L
TransportationOrderBooking Confirmation_In	To confirm a freight booking in your transportation management system
TransportationOrderBooking CancellationRequest_Out	To cancel a freight booking in your SAP BN4L
TransportationOrderBooking WaybillNotification_Out	To enable freight booking waybill notification request in your SAP BN4L

These interfaces manage every stage of a freight booking life cycle—from creating the booking request (_Request_Out) to confirming it back (_Confirmation_In). The cancellation message ensures flexibility in case of booking errors or plan changes, while the waybill notification enables regulatory or operational updates tied to the transport.

Freight Orders for Reporting interface

For businesses that rely on milestone-based tracking, SAP BN4L enables automated milestone reporting for freight orders. This allows visibility into critical transport events such as departures, arrivals, or customs clearance—automated via system communication instead of manual updates.

To achieve this, SAP TM or TM in S/4HANA sends or receives milestone-related data using the interface listed below.

Table 3-4. *GTT reporting interface*

Interface	Purpose
TransportationEventBulkNotification_In	To receive event notifications for freight orders from SAP BN4L

This interface ensures that freight orders are continuously updated with event-related information, allowing logistics planners and stakeholders to monitor the real-time status of shipments. For instance, it can record when a truck departs a warehouse or when it is delayed en route.

Track Freight Movement

SAP BN4L also supports live tracking of freight movements. This capability becomes especially powerful when carriers provide real-time data either via integration with visibility platforms or through manual reporting. The data collected can be viewed directly in the **Track Freight Movement** app or within SAP TM.

The system supports two key methods of tracking:

- **Automated Real-Time visibility**: Via integration with external visibility providers.

- **Manual Event Entry**: Carriers update milestones themselves using apps like Freight Orders for Reporting.

To make this work, your SAP system must be able to send tracking requests and receive updates using the following interfaces.

Table 3-5. *GTT sending and receiving interface*

Interface	Purpose
TransportationOrderGeneric TrackedProcessRequest_Out	To send requests for process tracking to SAP BN4L
TransportationEventBulk Notification_In	To receive event notifications for freight documents from SAP BN4L

The tracking request (GenericTrackedProcessRequest_Out) is typically sent once the transport order is ready and needs to be monitored. In return, SAP BN4L processes the actual updates—such as location changes, delay notices, or delivery confirmations—via the EventBulkNotification_In interface. This ensures the central system always reflects the current execution status.

By leveraging these interfaces across tendering, subcontracting, reporting, and tracking, companies can achieve high automation, reduce delays, and ensure accurate logistics visibility—directly within their SAP logistics landscape.

Web Portal

BN4L comes with a web portal that carriers can use to collaborate with shippers.

SAP BN4L features a dedicated web portal specifically designed to streamline collaboration between carriers and shippers. This digital platform presents an intuitive and accessible interface, making it easy for carriers to oversee their logistics partnerships and manage transport-related activities. The portal equips carriers with real-time access to essential shipment data, allowing them to review delivery details, confirm schedules, and engage in timely transaction handling.

One of the standout aspects of this web portal is its ability to support live updates on shipping progress, enabling carriers to provide immediate status changes, monitor ongoing deliveries, and maintain direct lines of communication with shipping partners. This direct engagement ensures smooth synchronization between parties, helping to eliminate delays and reduce miscommunication.

By offering a centralized environment for coordination, the portal reduces the complexity of logistics interactions. It also enhances transparency across the supply chain and contributes to more efficient workflows. Ultimately, the web portal improves the experience for both carriers and shippers by making day-to-day operations more manageable, collaborative, and effective.

EDI Integration

While, currently, API is the primary method for integration, SAP is working on providing additional endpoints (like EDIFACT and ANSI) for carriers to use.

At present, the main method for linking carriers with the SAP BN4L system is through API-based integration. However, SAP is actively developing support for additional connection formats such as EDIFACT and ANSI, which are widely recognized standards in the Electronic Data Interchange (EDI) domain. These new endpoints will offer carriers the ability to transmit structured logistics data electronically in formats that align with long-established industry protocols.

The inclusion of EDIFACT and ANSI will enable smoother interactions between shippers and carriers, particularly for organizations relying on older or existing EDI systems. This development reflects SAP's effort to increase compatibility with a broader range of logistics systems and to support varying levels of digital maturity among partners.

By broadening the integration options, SAP ensures that more companies—regardless of their current IT infrastructure—can seamlessly adopt and benefit from BN4L. This move will not only simplify integration for carriers accustomed to traditional data formats but will also enhance collaboration across the logistics ecosystem. Ultimately, these enhancements are designed to boost communication efficiency and interoperability across different platforms, making BN4L more adaptable and inclusive for the global logistics community.

Outbound Integration

When there's a change or business event in the SAP Transportation Management (TM) system, it triggers a call to BN4L, which then routes the information to the specific carrier's webhook based on the configuration.

In the SAP BN4L framework, outbound integration plays a crucial role in maintaining a continuous flow of information between the SAP Transportation Management (TM) system and external logistics partners. Whenever a key event—such as a shipment update, order modification, or transportation-related change—occurs within the SAP TM environment, a predefined trigger activates a communication call to BN4L. This system then intelligently forwards the necessary details to the correct carrier's webhook, using configurations defined during setup.

This automated flow ensures that carriers receive critical updates in real time, allowing them to swiftly react, make operational adjustments, and keep their data synchronized with that of the shipper. As a result, processes such as rescheduling, status changes, or route optimization can be initiated without delay.

By removing the need for manual data transmission, this outbound integration significantly boosts the efficiency of logistics operations. It minimizes human error, increases the precision of shared information, and fosters tighter alignment between shippers and their carrier partners.

This streamlined communication mechanism strengthens supply chain responsiveness and ensures that all stakeholders remain informed and agile.

Inbound Integration

Carriers can also initiate communication by calling BN4L's APIs, which then routes the data to the appropriate system.

Beyond supporting outbound integration, SAP BN4L also facilitates inbound data exchange, empowering carriers to proactively communicate with the platform. Through dedicated API endpoints, carriers can push essential updates—such as shipment progress, delivery confirmations, or changes in transport status—directly into the BN4L system.

Upon receiving this data, BN4L intelligently processes and channels it to the appropriate downstream system, such as SAP Transportation Management or any other integrated back-end application, based on the predefined routing logic. This ensures that all relevant stakeholders receive timely and accurate information without any manual handoffs.

This two-way integration not only supports real-time collaboration between logistics partners but also enables a synchronized flow of communication. Carriers can keep their shipper counterparts continuously informed, reducing uncertainty and enhancing the overall coordination of supply chain activities. The result is improved transparency, faster decision-making, and more agile responses to dynamic logistics scenarios, all contributing to a more resilient and streamlined supply chain network.

SOAMANAGER and WeBSERVICE Configuration

SOA Manager (SOAMANAGER) is a browser-accessible utility designed to control and set up the way SAP systems connect and interact with other software platforms within a service-based framework. Refer to Figure 3-1 for a visual representation. This tool plays a key role in managing how services—such as web services—are structured and used within the SAP environment. It helps administrators configure communication pathways between SAP and outside systems, especially when these systems rely on different integration standards like SOAP, REST, or similar communication protocols. Essentially, SOAMANAGER acts as the central control point for defining, maintaining, and monitoring service-based connections in a distributed SAP architecture.

Figure 3-1. *SOAMANAGER application screen*

Key functions and features of SOAMANAGER include

1. **Web Service Configuration:** SOAMANAGER acts as the command center for managing web services in an SAP environment. Think of it as the place where service interfaces are brought to life and made functional for business communication. Administrators can define which services are active, deactivate outdated services, and customize service behaviors to suit specific scenarios. It supports both system-to-system and user-facing service configurations, offering flexible control over service visibility and availability. For example, in a multi-tenant landscape, you can configure the same service differently for different clients or business units.

2. **Security Settings:** This is one of the most critical aspects of SOAMANAGER. Security here isn't just about passwords—it involves a layered approach:

    *   **Authentication:** Establishes *who* is calling the service. You can configure simple username-password pairs for internal use or digital certificates (via STRUST) for secure machine-to-machine communication.

    *   **Authorization:** Determines *what* the service consumer is allowed to do once authenticated. Role-based restrictions can prevent unintended access or misuse.

- **Encryption:** Protects the data *in transit*. Whether using SSL or WS-Security headers, encryption ensures sensitive business data—such as logistics orders, pricing, or customer records—remains unreadable to outsiders during transmission.

  SAP also lets you manage policy templates so that multiple services can follow consistent security guidelines, reducing administrative overhead and errors.

3. **Endpoint Management**

   Every web service in SAP needs a target location—a URL where it listens or sends data. SOAMANAGER makes managing these "endpoints" very systematic. Whether you're connecting to a third-party logistics provider or to another SAP system in a hybrid landscape, SOAMANAGER ensures that endpoints are accurately configured with the correct URL, port, and protocol.

   You can

   - Assign multiple endpoints to a single service to support different use cases (e.g., testing, production, disaster recovery)

   - Bind the service to specific protocols like SOAP 1.1 or 1.2 based on the consumer's capability

   - Add message-level options like compression, response timeout, and retry behavior to make communication more resilient

4. **Communication Monitoring**

After services are live, SOAMANAGER allows administrators to observe how these services perform in real-world conditions. This isn't just about logs—it's about deep visibility.

- You can trace the exact payload of a request that failed, including headers, body, and errors returned.

- It helps you detect if the service failed due to incorrect parameters, timeout, or access restrictions.

- With tools like **SRT_MONI**, SAP offers a timeline view of request processing, showing each step and potential delays.

  This monitoring functionality helps isolate problems faster, especially in integration-heavy environments where services may depend on one another.

5. **Service Consumer Configuration**

SOAMANAGER is not only for hosting services—it also allows SAP to act as a **consumer**. This means your SAP system can call external APIs, such as a courier tracking system, payment gateway, or even a cloud analytics engine.

- Logical ports are used to define how SAP should connect to these external services.

- Security configurations (e.g., OAuth tokens, SSL certificates) are tied directly to these ports.

- The tool allows the import of external WSDL files to define the expected service structure, enabling SAP to correctly format and send requests.

To activate the TransportationOrderGenericTrackedProcessRequest_ out or any other BN4L web service in SAP through SOAMANAGER, you will need to follow a series of steps. These steps typically involve locating the specific web service, configuring it, and ensuring it's properly activated for use.

Step 1: Access SOAMANAGER

1. Begin by logging into your SAP system using valid credentials that grant access to system administration tools.

2. In the SAP GUI, enter the transaction code / nSOAMANAGER into the command input field and press **Enter**. This action will open a browser-based interface in a new tab or window, redirecting you to the SOAMANAGER application.

🔍 *Tip*   *Make sure that your user role has the necessary authorizations for SOA configuration tasks. Otherwise, access to some features might be restricted.*

Step 2: Find the Web Service

1. Within SOAMANAGER, look for the **"Web Service Configuration"** section. This may be found directly on the homepage or in the navigation menu, depending on the version of SAP NetWeaver in use.

2. Under this configuration area, select **"Manage Services"** or **"Find Services."** These functions allow you to search for existing web services that are available but not yet activated.

3. In the search panel, type the exact name of the web service interface you're targeting, for example:

    TransportationOrderGenericTrackedProcessRequest_out

4. Click the **Search** button to display matching services. Once found, confirm that it matches the expected namespace and interface definition to avoid confusion with similarly named services.

Step 3: Activate the Web Service

1. When the TransportationOrderGenericTracked ProcessRequest_out service appears in the results list, select it. This will take you to the service details screen, where you can view metadata and technical configurations.

2. Click the **Activate** or **Create Service** button, depending on the system version. This action publishes the web service and prepares it to be called externally.

    - At this stage, the system might generate a WSDL URL automatically, which defines the structure and usage of the service.

💡 *Behind the scenes, activation registers the service's endpoint, binds it to communication settings, and prepares it to accept calls.*

Step 4: Configure the Web Service

1. **Configure Security**: This is a crucial step to safeguard your service.

   - Define authentication method: choose between basic authentication (username/password), SAML, or digital certificates.

   - If your endpoint requires HTTPS, make sure SSL is enabled and the correct certificate is installed in STRUST.

   - Consider configuring message-level security using WS-Security if the consumer expects encrypted payloads.

2. **Define Endpoint**: This is where you specify the target system or network location that the web service will use.

   - Typically, the system will generate a default endpoint (URL), but you should review it and customize if needed (e.g., adding load balancer URLs or external DNS paths).

3. **Select Binding Type**

   - You must define how the web service should communicate.

   - Choose between **SOAP 1.1**, **SOAP 1.2**, or other bindings based on the client's requirements. This affects how headers and payloads are handled.

   - Assign appropriate message protocol versions and transport methods (HTTP/HTTPS).

✹ *Advanced systems may also configure logging levels, performance thresholds, or quality of service settings at this point.*

Step 5: Test the Web Service

1. After activation and configuration, it's important to validate functionality before going live.

2. Use the **"Test"** feature in SOAMANAGER (if available for your service). This lets you simulate service calls by entering dummy data and observing the system response.

   - You'll be prompted to enter request payload parameters—ensure these conform to the expected XML schema.

   - Successful tests indicate that the web service is accessible and behaving as intended.

🔄 *If errors occur during testing, revisit endpoint settings and authentication credentials, or check system logs for deeper analysis.*

Step 6: Monitor the Web Service (Optional)

1. To ensure long-term reliability, you should actively monitor service calls.

2. Use transactions like SXI_MONITOR or SOAMANAGER's own monitoring tools to inspect

   - Message logs

   - Faults and exceptions

   - Performance metrics (e.g., latency, throughput)

📊 *Regular monitoring helps detect issues early—such as repeated failures from a specific partner system—before they affect operations.*

Step 7: Check for Dependencies (Optional)

- Confirm that any background infrastructure required by the service is in place:

  - **RFC destinations** for back-end connectivity

  - **Communication arrangements** in SAP S/4HANA Cloud

  - **PI/PO mappings** if middleware is involved

- If the service is part of a larger integration scenario (like GTT or TM), make sure those dependencies are not misconfigured or missing.

Step 8: Documentation and Alerts (Optional)

- Maintain documentation of all configuration steps for audits, support, and future changes.

- In production landscapes, it's smart to set up **alerts** or automated monitoring rules that notify admins of failures or slowdowns.

  - This can include email alerts, SAP Solution Manager integration, or even third-party tools like Splunk or ELK Stack.

📝 *Well-documented and monitored web services reduce the risk of unplanned outages and make onboarding new partners easier.*

✅ Final Thoughts

Once the TransportationOrderGenericTrackedProcessRequest_out service is fully configured and tested, it's ready for real-world use. Whether it's sending updates about shipment orders or synchronizing logistics data across networks, SOAMANAGER ensures secure and reliable connectivity.

Figure 3-2. *SOAMANAGER web service screen*

Figure 3-3. *SOAMANAGER web service screen*

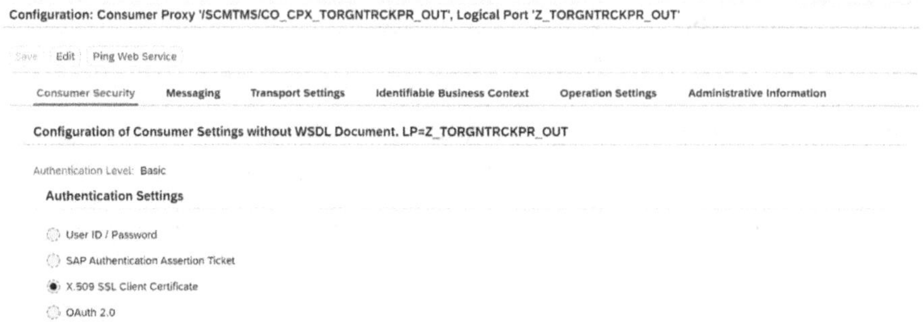

Configuration: Consumer Proxy '/SCMTMS/CO_CPX_TORGNTRCKPR_OUT', Logical Port 'Z_TORGNTRCKPR_OUT'

Save   Edit   Ping Web Service

Consumer Security   Messaging   Transport Settings   Identifiable Business Context   Operation Settings   Administrative Information

Configuration of Consumer Settings without WSDL Document. LP=Z_TORGNTRCKPR_OUT

Authentication Level: Basic

Authentication Settings

○ User ID / Password

○ SAP Authentication Assertion Ticket

◉ X.509 SSL Client Certificate

○ OAuth 2.0

Figure 3-4. *SOAMANAGER web service screen*

Overall, SOAMANAGER simplifies the configuration and management of web services, enabling seamless integration between SAP and other systems in a service-oriented environment. It is typically used by SAP basis administrators, developers, and integrators to set up, maintain, and troubleshoot web services in SAP systems.

About the Core Engine

The core engine (Figure 3-5) is a central part of SAP BN4L and Global Track and Trace. It provides functionality for process tracking and event handling that is common to all tracking applications independent of their original business domain. In particular, the core engine provides the following:

- A common definition of tracked processes and events that are enhanced with business domain specifics by each application

- A common ingestion pipeline for initial creation and updates of tracked process instances

- A common ingestion pipeline for processing actual events and identifying affected tracked process instances

- A common service to query tracked processes and related events

The ingestion pipelines for tracked process instances and actual events are realized as RESTful services that can be called for example from SAP Cloud Integration. The service to query tracked process instances and events related to these instances is realized with the OData protocol for RESTful services. Figure 3-5 shows the integration of the core engine with application-specific services and UIs and existing ERP systems leveraging SAP Cloud Integration.

At the heart of SAP BN4L and its Global Track and Trace (GTT) functionality lies the **core engine**, a robust service layer that provides foundational capabilities for tracking logistics processes and managing the flow of real-time events. The engine is designed to operate independently of specific industries or supply chain structures, offering a versatile base on which specialized applications are built.

1. **Key Functions of the Core Engine**

   - **Standardized Definitions for Tracking Entities**

     The engine uses a unified model to define tracked business processes (e.g., a shipment or purchase order) and associated events (e.g., pickup, loading, customs clearance). Each BN4L or GTT application can build on this core structure by adding domain-specific data relevant to its use case.

- **Ingestion of Process Instances**

  The engine has a shared input pipeline used to
  create or update instances of logistics processes.
  For example, when a new freight order is created
  in SAP TM, the pipeline registers it in the core
  engine so it can be monitored in real time.

- **Ingestion of Actual Events**

  Separate from process creation, this pipeline is
  used for receiving real-world updates, such as
  GPS location changes, sensor data, or scanned
  shipping documents. These events are matched
  with the appropriate tracked process instance,
  triggering status updates and alerts.

- **Query Service for Data Retrieval**

  The engine provides a standardized querying
  capability. This allows users and applications
  to retrieve up-to-date information about
  shipments, processes, and historical event logs.
  This query service is crucial for dashboards,
  analytics, and user interfaces that present
  logistics insights.

2. **Technical Implementation of the Core Engine**

- **REST-Based Ingestion Pipelines**

  Both the creation/update of tracked processes and
  the submission of real-world events are handled
  through RESTful services. These are typically called
  by middleware tools such as SAP Cloud Integration,
  which connects source systems like SAP S/4HANA
  or external carrier platforms.

- **OData for Querying**

  For fetching data—such as current shipment status or event history—the core engine leverages the OData protocol. This REST-compliant approach makes it easy to embed tracking data into external apps, reporting tools, or custom-built dashboards.

3. **System Integration View (Figure 3-5 Conceptual Description)**

   The diagram (Figure 3-5) conceptually illustrates how the core engine acts as a central hub. On one side, it connects to various SAP systems (like SAP TM, S/4HANA, and Event Management), and on the other, it links with domain-specific apps through the cloud. The engine interacts with both user-facing interfaces and technical services, enabling a fully connected and transparent logistics workflow.

4. **Why the Core Engine Matters**

   The core engine simplifies and unifies how logistics tracking is executed across multiple systems, business partners, and transport modes. It offers a flexible yet standardized way to

   - Aggregate data from multiple sources

   - React to real-world logistics events in real time

   - Provide transparency and control through a single data model

   - Support custom tracking logic with reusable components

Together with master data, this architecture makes SAP BN4L a powerful platform for digital logistics collaboration.

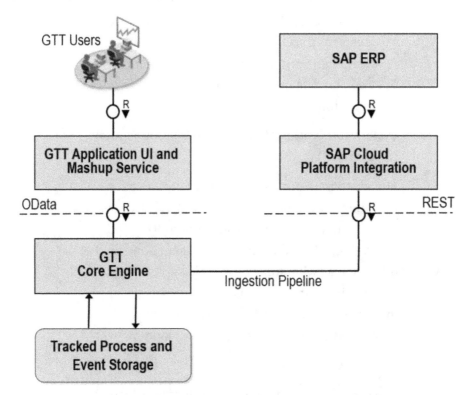

Figure 3-5. *SAP Global Track and Trace integration*

APIs and Interfaces

There are two basic types of API:

- **Public Cross-tenant APIs**: These are published by SAP in the SAP Business Accelerator Hub with documentation.

- **Generated Tenant-Local Interfaces**: These are also APIs but to easily distinguish them for SAP BN4L Global Track and Trace, we call them interfaces. They are documented in this guide.

1. **APIs and Interfaces in SAP BN4L**

    SAP BN4L relies on system interfaces and APIs
    to connect participants and streamline logistics
    operations. These digital connectors allow
    the safe and structured flow of data between
    different systems. Two distinct types of integration
    points exist:

    1. **Public Cross-tenant APIs**

        These APIs are made available by SAP
        and are accessible from the SAP Business
        Accelerator Hub. They allow systems outside
        of your organization to connect with SAP
        BN4L. Typically used when shippers, carriers, or
        service providers from different organizations
        need to collaborate, these APIs are standardized
        and documented to promote seamless external
        integration.

    2. **Generated Tenant-Local Interfaces**

        These are custom-built integration points
        generated within a specific customer's
        environment. They're mainly used for internal
        communication within the tenant's system,
        especially in use cases such as SAP Global Track
        and Trace. While technically APIs, they are
        referred to as "interfaces" for clarity and are kept
        private to the organization's network.

2. **The Core Model and How It Ties into APIs and Interfaces**

SAP BN4L is built on a core model that defines essential logistics data types and their relationships. This model acts as a template for how information—such as shipment details or carrier assignments—is structured and shared.

- **Custom Models from the Core**

  Businesses can create models tailored to their operations. These define which types of logistics data will be exchanged, such as delivery checkpoints or vehicle updates.

- **Deployment and Interface Generation**

  Once models are finalized, they are activated in the system. At this point, system-generated interfaces are created, allowing read/write access to the model's data—enabling actions like sending status updates or receiving order confirmations.

- **Unified Data Structure**

  The core model ensures that all systems interpret logistics data the same way. For instance, the connection between a delivery and its assigned truck is clearly defined, enabling better coordination and reducing inconsistencies in data handling.

3. **How This All Comes Together**

Here's a breakdown of how the different components—APIs, interfaces, and models—interact to streamline operations in SAP BN4L:

1. **Define and Deploy Core Models**

   Users begin by identifying which logistics entities matter to their business (like shipments or carriers). These models are then deployed in the system.

2. **Generate Interfaces**

   Upon deployment, the system automatically provides interfaces to access and update the model data. These allow real-time communication about milestones, shipment status, and related events.

3. **Integrate APIs and Interfaces**

   Depending on whether the communication is internal or across organizations, the system uses either public APIs or tenant-specific interfaces. External APIs support collaboration with partners, while interfaces are ideal for internal process flows.

4. **Maintain Continuous Data Flow**

   Once the system is integrated, data such as tracking updates, shipment progress, and event alerts move fluidly between all participants—keeping everyone on the same page in real time.

5.   **Use Core Entities to Guide Logistics Decisions**

With the core model serving as a shared language, different systems can better understand how shipment, carrier, and event data relate. This allows teams to make quick, informed decisions—for example, rerouting a delivery in response to a delay or assigning a new subcontractor if needed.

By the end of this overview, it becomes clear how SAP BN4L's architecture—powered by structured models, APIs, and interfaces—provides a robust platform for digital collaboration. The result is greater efficiency, improved coordination, and the ability to act proactively within an ever-changing logistics landscape.

Core Model You can define models based on the core model. After model deployment, read/write interfaces can be generated. Core entities are shared by every model. Their relationships are shown in Figure 3-6.

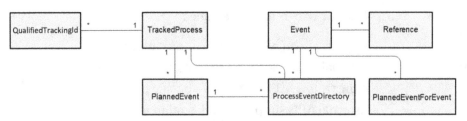

Figure 3-6. *Core model*

Master Data Maintenance

Master data is a critical component for the effective functioning of SAP BN4L and SAP GTT. It ensures that all systems and processes are aligned, enabling seamless integration and efficient operations. Here's an overview of the master data required for both platforms.

Master Data in SAP BN4L

The following provides an overview of the master data required for SAP BN4L.

- **Business Partners**

  In order to enable interaction within the logistics network, all participants—such as freight carriers, shipping companies, and logistics service firms—need to be registered as business partners in the system. Each participant is assigned specific roles (e.g., "Carrier" or "Shipper") that determine their function and interaction rules within SAP BN4L. These role assignments are essential for routing workflows and communications correctly.

- **Locations**

  Logistical points such as warehouses, ports, hubs, and distribution centers need to be clearly defined in the system. Each location record should include accurate coordinates and address details. This data supports route planning, tracking accuracy, and efficient allocation of transportation resources.

- **Transportation Resources**

  The system requires structured information about transportation assets—trucks, trailers, containers, and related equipment. Details such as carrying capacity, equipment specifications, and availability help in planning and optimizing the use of these assets across logistics operations.

- **Freight Agreements**

  Agreements between transport service providers
  and shippers, including negotiated freight rates and
  contractual terms, are captured in this master data
  category. These agreements define the cost structure,
  service levels, and other legal or operational
  conditions that apply during logistics execution.

- **Products and Materials**

  Goods being moved through the logistics network
  must be identified with detailed material data. This
  includes size, weight, packaging specifications, and
  any special handling instructions. Maintaining this
  information supports proper vehicle allocation, safety
  compliance, and load optimization.

- **Event Types**

  Standardized event definitions are necessary to
  monitor progress throughout the transport life cycle.
  Examples include events like "Goods Picked Up," "In
  Transit," "Arrived at Destination," and "Delivered."
  These predefined milestones support real-time status
  tracking and exception handling across all stages of
  shipment execution.

Master Data in SAP GTT

- **Business Partners**

  - Similar to BN4L, business partners such as
    shippers, carriers, and customers must be defined.

  - Roles and responsibilities are assigned to ensure
    proper event reporting and tracking.

- **Products:** Detailed information about the products being tracked, including serial numbers, batch numbers, and other identifiers

- **Locations:** Comprehensive data about origin, destination, and intermediate locations for shipments

- **Event Types and Milestones**

  - Customizable event types for tracking planned, actual, and unplanned events.

  - Examples include "Departure," "Arrival," "Delay," and "Exception."

- **Integration Data**

  - Configuration for integrating with SAP TM, SAP S/4HANA, and external systems

  - Includes API endpoints, EDI configurations, and data mapping rules

- **Visibility Providers:** Information about third-party visibility providers integrated with GTT for real-time tracking

DRFOUT: Location Master Creation to BN4L Using Data Replication Framework

You can use the **Manage Locations** app to manage location master data, which was manually copied or replicated from SAP S/4HANA or created from new using the app. Location master data can then be used by the **System Connections** app in SAP BN4L Global Track and Trace. There are two master data maintenance in BN4L: Location Master and Carrier BP Creation. This section provides explains how to configure a system when used in conjunction with the relevant master data.

Note   In SAP TM and SAP BN4L, any type of location, whether it's a shipping point, carrier, or plant, is considered a location. This modal will be applicable on all the location setup.

Location Data

Location master data interface ***LocationBulkReplicationRequest_Out*** (Figure 3-7) needs to be created in TM system to support data replication via DRF. It is not pre-delivered as part of SAP TM 9.6 version.

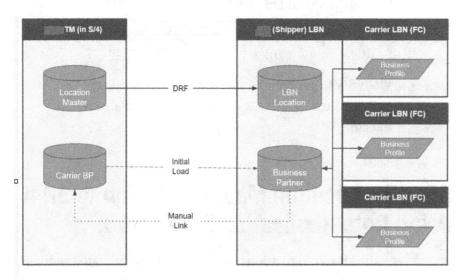

Figure 3-7. DRF framework

LocationBulkReplicationRequest_Out is an asynchronous inbound service in SAP BN4L. It allows shippers to replicate location master data from an external system to SAP BN4L. Here's a brief overview:

1. **Service Type**: Asynchronous inbound service.

2. **Purpose**: To replicate location master data from an external system to SAP BN4L.

3. **Interface**: Uses a SOAP interface to transmit the business data for location replication.

4. **Data Structure**: The interface includes a bulk service message header and individual location replication request messages, which contain location IDs, location type codes, descriptions, and address fields.

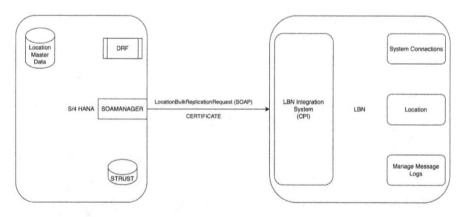

Figure 3-8. *DRF and SOAMANAGER integration*

Figure 3-9. *Location interface and fields*

Once the service interface is created, class needs to be created to send location master data from TM to BN4L using DRFOUT transaction

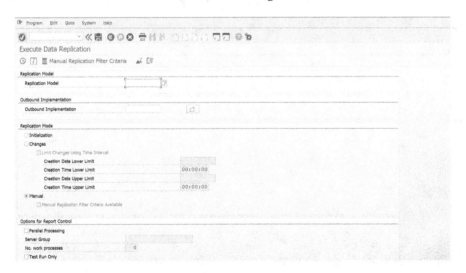

Figure 3-10. *DRFOUT (T code) screen*

DRFOUT process of Data Replication Framework Output (DRFOUT), which is a key component in managing location master data. This process plays a crucial role in ensuring that location-related information is accurately replicated across different SAP systems, enabling seamless data synchronization and consistency.

Location master data encompasses critical information about physical and organizational locations, such as warehouses, plants, distribution centers, shipping points, and more. This data is essential for various logistics, planning, and execution processes across the enterprise, and ensuring its accuracy and consistency is vital for efficient operations.

The DRFOUT process specifically handles the output of location master data, ensuring that it is transmitted from the source system to the target systems where it is required for further processing or use. This ensures that all systems involved in the supply chain or transportation management have up-to-date and accurate location information, reducing the risk of errors and improving operational efficiency.

Manual Master Data Maintenance: Manage Locations App

The **SAP Manage Locations** app is a powerful tool designed to streamline the management of location master data within SAP TM (Transportation Management) and SAP BN4L. Whether you are working with shipping points, carriers, or plants, the app allows you to efficiently maintain location details, whether they are manually entered or replicated from external systems. This is essential for ensuring accurate and up-to-date location information for logistics and supply chain operations.

In this chapter, we will explore the functionality of the SAP Manage Locations app, focusing on its role in data management and integration with other SAP applications. By the end of this chapter, you will be familiar with how to navigate the app, input location data, and leverage it for various logistics operations.

The following key features will be covered:

- **Manual Master Data Maintenance**: How to manually manage location data within the app

- **Integration with Docking Location Settings**: How the app interacts with other logistics functions, such as docking location management

- **Location Data Creation**: Steps for creating new locations from scratch within the app

- **Replicating Location Data**: How location data can be replicated from other systems

The SAP Manage Locations app is used to manage location master data either manually replicated from another system or created from scratch using the app. It can be consumed by other apps, such as Docking Location Settings in SAP BN4L Freight Collaboration. The app is part of the Master Data Maintenance app, which also includes other functionality related to technical assets and maintenance objects.

You can access the SAP Manage Locations app in the SAP BN4L Shipper Tenant by following these steps:

1. Go to the SAP BN4L Shipper Tenant.

2. Click on the **"Master Data"** section in the main menu.

3. Then, click **"Manage Locations"** to open the location master data management interface.

This will allow you to begin managing and maintaining your location data within SAP BN4L.

The data in these features consists of not only the address information but also the business purpose of a location. To add or edit information to any field got you need to accesses the

Additionally, the master data of a location can include one or more alternative IDs so that the location becomes cross-platform identifiable. It can then be consumed by other apps in SAP BN4L Global Track and Trace. In the following sections, you'll see how to navigate through each page and update information as needed.

View a Location

Display Location Fiori Screen: Overview and Purpose

The **Display Location Fiori screen** in SAP BN4L is a key tool used to manage and display location master data. It enables you to add and edit information related to various location attributes such as Location ID, External ID, Object Type, Source, Description, Country/Region, State, and City. This feature is essential for maintaining accurate location data, which can be used across various logistics operations, including dock appointments, freight order management, and network integration.

What You Will Do in This Section

In this section, you will learn how to access the **Display Location** screen and utilize the settings button to manage the location attributes. You will walk through the steps of updating or adding new data in the relevant fields, ensuring that your location master data is accurate and up-to-date.

Steps to Access and Use the Display Location Fiori Screen

1. **Go to the SAP BN4L Shipper Tenant**

   - Open your SAP BN4L system in the browser and log in using your credentials.

2. **Navigate to the "Master Data" Section**

   - On the main dashboard, click the **"Master Data"** tab located in the main navigation menu.

3. **Select the "Manage Locations" Option**

   - In the drop-down or list of options under "Master Data," click **"Manage Locations."** This will take you to the **Display Location** screen.

4. **Access the Display Location Fiori Screen**

   - You will now be on the **Display Location** screen where you can view existing location data or add new locations. The screen should be displayed with various fields, including Location ID, External ID, Object Type, Source, Description, Country/Region, State, and City.

5. **Click the Settings Button to Edit the Location Data**

   - To add or modify information in the fields, click the **Settings button** (typically represented by a gear icon) found at the top or side of the screen.

6. **Edit or Add Information to Location Fields**

   - Once the Settings button is clicked, you can begin editing the following fields:

     - **Location ID**: Assign or update the unique identifier for the location.

     - **External ID**: Add an external reference ID, if necessary.

     - **Object Type**: Select the type of location (e.g., shipping point, plant, etc.).

     - **Source**: Specify the source of the location data.

     - **Description**: Provide a short description of the location.

     - **Country/Region**: Select the country or region where the location is situated.

     - **State**: Specify the state or province of the location.

     - **City**: Enter the city where the location is based.

7. **Save Your Changes**

   - After entering or editing the necessary information, click **Save** to update the location data.

Key Screens to Note:

- **Display Location Fiori Screen (Caption 1)**: This is where you will initially view and manage location information.

- **Settings Screen (Caption 2)**: Accessed via the settings button to modify and update location fields.

By following these steps, you will be able to efficiently manage and maintain your location master data in SAP BN4L, ensuring smooth logistics and network operations.

The Display Location Fiori screen is used to add

- Location ID

- External ID

- Object Type

- Source

- Description

- Country/Region

- State

- City

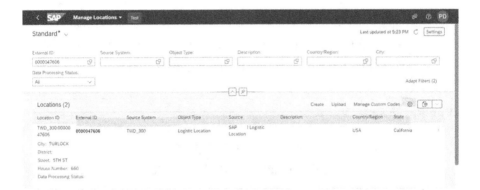

Figure 3-11. *Display Location Fiori screen*

Create a Location

The **Create a Location** feature in SAP BN4L allows you to add new
locations to your system, essential for managing various logistics
operations like freight orders, dock appointments, and location-specific
activities. This feature enables you to define key attributes for each
location, such as its ID, External ID, Object Type, Description, Country/
Region, State, and City. Properly creating and managing locations
ensures that your logistics processes are accurately mapped to real-world
geographic locations, improving communication, coordination, and
operational efficiency.

What You Will Do in This Section

In this section, you will learn how to access the **Create Location** screen,
input relevant details for a new location, and save the newly created
location to the system. You will walk through the steps of entering location
data such as Location ID, Object Type, and Description, and you will
understand the importance of each field in creating a valid location record.

Steps to Create a Location

1. **Go to the SAP BN4L Shipper Tenant**

   - Open your SAP BN4L system in your browser, and log in with your credentials.

2. **Navigate to the "Master Data" Section**

   - On the main dashboard, click the **"Master Data"** tab located in the navigation menu.

3. **Select the "Manage Locations" Option**

   - From the "Master Data" section, click **"Manage Locations."** This will open the screen where you can create and manage locations.

4. **Click the "Create Location" Button**

   - On the **Manage Locations** screen, click the **"Create Location"** button, which is usually located at the top or in a prominent area of the page.

5. **Fill in the Location Details**

   - You will be taken to the **Create Location** screen, where you will input details for the new location. The fields include

     - **Location ID**: Enter a unique identifier for the location.

     - **External ID**: Optionally, you can add an external reference ID if applicable.

     - **Object Type**: Choose the type of location (e.g., shipping point, carrier, or plant).

- **Source**: Indicate where the location data is coming from (if applicable).

- **Description**: Provide a clear description of the location.

- **Country/Region:** Select the country or region for this location.

- **State**: Specify the state or province of the location.

- **City**: Enter the city for the location.

6. **Save the Location**

- Once all the required fields are filled out, click **Save** to create and save the location in the system.

Key Screens to Note:

- **Create Location Screen** (Figure 3-12): This is where you will enter all the details for the new location.

- **Manage Locations Screen** (Figure 3-12): After creating a location, you will return to this screen to view or further manage the location data.

By following these steps, you will successfully create a new location in SAP BN4L, allowing for better management and coordination of logistics activities.

Steps to Create a Location

1. Click Create on the upper-right corner of the Locations table. The Create New Location page opens.

Figure 3-12. *Create Location Fiori screen*

- Source: Source of the location.

- Location Type: This field is available when Source is set to SAP SCM Logistic Location.

Figure 3-13. *Create Location Fiori screen (field entry)*

- Source System/External ID: Source system from which the location master data is copied and the corresponding ID.

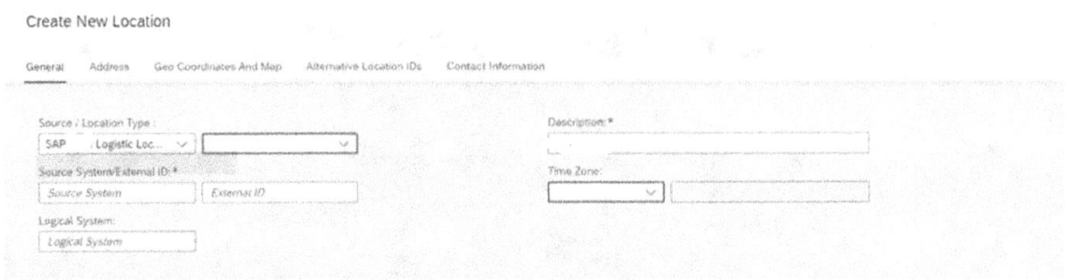

Create New Location

General   Address   Geo Coordinates And Map   Alternative Location IDs   Contact Information

Source / Location Type :
SAP   . Logistic Loc...

Source System/External ID: *
Source System   External ID

Logical System:
Logical System

Description: *

Time Zone:

Figure 3-14. *Create Location Fiori screen (field entry)*

If you are creating a location from scratch, set the Source System part to LBN, and set the External ID part to the location ID you previously specified.

If you are importing a location from SAP Transportation Management (TM), set the Source System to the business system name of your TM system, and set the External ID to the location ID in TM.

- Longitude: Longitude coordinate of the location
- Latitude: Latitude coordinate of the location
  - Country/Region
  - State
  - City
  - District
  - Street/House Number
  - Zip Code
  - Time Zone

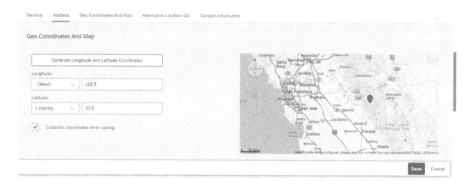

Figure 3-15. *Create Location Fiori screen (geo-coordinates field entry)*

Mass Upload Locations

Figure 3-16. *Mass upload location Fiori screen*

1. Download the Excel template available by choosing
   the Download Excel Template button.

Figure 3-17. *Mass upload location Fiori screen*

2. Fill the details of the locations you want to upload in the template.

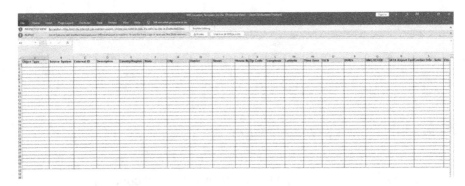

Figure 3-18. *Mass Excel upload location Fiori screen*

3. Choose Upload Locations to upload the modified Excel template.

Figure 3-19. *Mass Excel upload location Fiori screen*

Edit a Location

1. Use the following fields to filter locations:

    - Location ID

    - Description

    - Location Type

    - Country/Region

    - City

2. Click the location from the filter results to open the details page.

3. Choose Edit on the upper-right corner of the details page.

Figure 3-20. *Location Fiori screen*

Manage Custom Codes

You can use the manage custom codes feature to extend the drop-down list for the following fields:

- Country/Region

- State

- Location Type

- Time Zone

- Role of Contact

Figure 3-21. *Location Fiori screen (Manage custom code)*

This feature is useful if the drop-down list of a field does not contain the code you want to select. For example, you do not find the region code you need in the drop-down list of Country/Region.

Choose the Manage Custom Codes button.

On the Manage Custom Codes page, select the field for which you want to extend the list, and then, choose Create.

Specify the name, language, and description of the code, and then, choose Save.

Figure 3-22. Location Fiori screen

Generate Geo-Coordinates

The longitude and latitude coordinates of a location record can be maintained both manually and automatically.

To manually set the geo-coordinates for a location record, switch to the Geo Coordinates and Map tab of the record, and then enter the coordinates in the Longitude and Latitude fields. If you want the system to verify your entries, select Calibrate coordinates when saving before you save your changes.

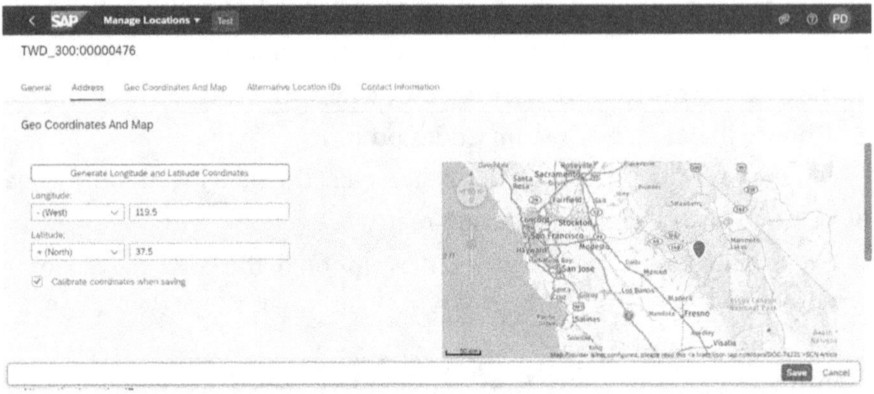

Figure 3-23. *Location Fiori screen (geo-coordinates entry)*

To have the system set the geo-coordinates for a location record, switch to the Geo Coordinates and Map tab of the record, and then, choose Generate Longitude and Latitude Coordinates. The system will generate the geo-coordinates according to the address you've entered. If you want the system to generate geo-coordinates for all the existing location records this way, you can turn the Generate geo-coordinates automatically setting on from the Settings dialog box, which can be found on the upper-right corner of the app home screen.

Figure 3-24. *Location Fiori screen*

Manage Entities

This feature is used to create Loading location, Docking Location, Gate, and Yard.

Loading Point

You can define the attributes of a loading point and manage the business hours and block time.

1. Choose the Loading Point tab on the left pane.

2. Choose the Add Loading Point button.

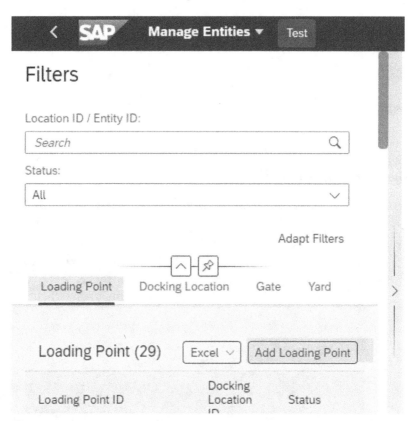

Figure 3-25. *Location Fiori screen*

3.   Define settings for the following sections:

    3.1.   Details

        • Location ID

        Select a location ID. You maintain location
        master data in the Manage Locations app.

Figure 3-26. *Location Fiori screen*

- Loading Point ID

Figure 3-27. Location Fiori screen

- Capacity

  Specify the number of loading/unloading activities that can be performed concurrently at the loading point.

Figure 3-28. *Location Fiori screen*

- Activity Type

  Specify whether you can perform loading,
  unloading, or both activities in this
  loading point.

Figure 3-29. *Location Fiori screen*

- Enable Appointment Date Change

    If you enable this indicator, the carriers can change
    the date of a dock appointment. You can specify
    a range for the loading point so that carriers can
    change the date within the specified range.

    Advance Up To

    Specify the number of days up to which the
    carrier can advance the dock appointment date.

    Postpone Up To

    Specify the number of days up to which the carrier
    can postpone the dock appointment date.

Figure 3-30. *Location Fiori screen*

- Enable Time Slot Setting

    If you enable time slot setting for this loading
    point, you can define the time slot duration for
    which this loading point can be booked. Note
    that this setting is enabled by default.

Time Slot

You can select a time slot duration for which the loading point can be booked. You can select up to six hours.

Figure 3-31. *Location Fiori screen (time details)*

- Overbooking Setting

  You can enable or disable overbooking for this loading point. When you enable overbooking, the system allows the user to book appointments even after the available slots are booked. If you enable this indicator, the system displays the following:

  Overbooking Limit

  If you enable the overbooking setting, you must specify the overbooking limit. Overbooking limit refers to the number of appointments that can be booked once the available slots are booked. Note that as of now, you can set the overbooking limit up to 50.

Enable Overbooking for Carriers

If you enable the overbooking setting, you must either enable or disable the overbooking option for the carriers. When you enable the overbooking option for carriers, the carriers can book appointments even after the available slots are booked. Note that the overbooking limit that you set here applies for the carriers as well when you enable this setting.

TWD_300:00000476   Edit   Deactivate   ⤢   ✕
TWD_300:00000476
                                        ⌄

Details   Business Hours (1)   Block Time (0)

Overbooking Details   **Assignment Details**

Enable Overbooking: Enable Assignment with Docking Locations:
Enabled   Disabled

Overbooking Limit:
5

Enable Overbooking for Carriers:
Disabled

Remarks:

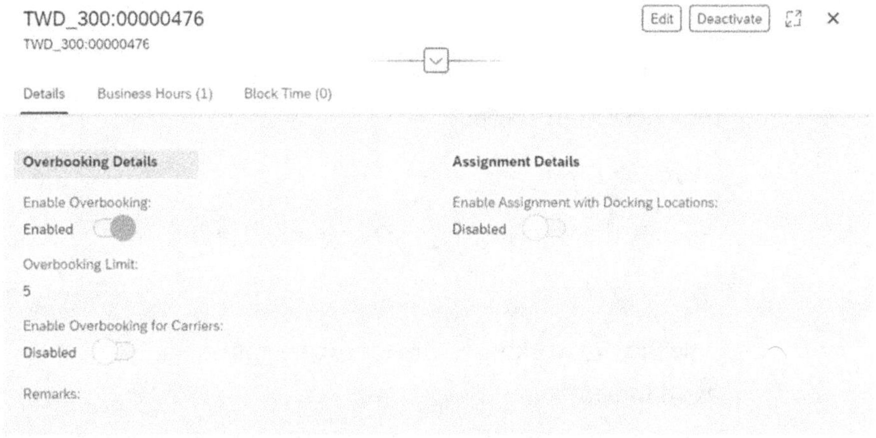

Figure 3-32. *Location Fiori screen*

- Enable Assignment with Docking Locations

  If you enable this setting, the loading point can be associated with multiple docking locations in the same time zone. If you disable this setting, the loading point can be associated with only one docking location in the same time zone.

- Assigned Docking Locations

  You can select the docking locations in the same time zone with which you want to share the loading point.

- Remarks

  You can enter the additional information about the loading point in this section.

- Business Hours

  Period

  Specify the duration for which the entry of business hours is valid.

  Working Days

  Specify the working days of the loading point.

  Working Hours

  Specify the working hours for the specified working days.

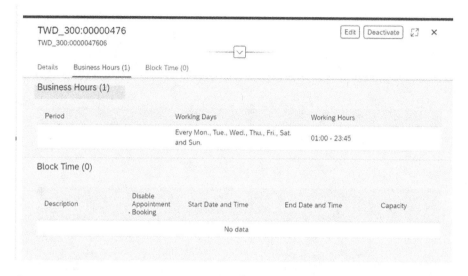

Figure 3-33. *Location Fiori screen (time details)*

- Deleting Business Hours

    To delete an entry of business hours, choose the delete icon that appears next to the entry. You can also choose Delete from the details pane that appears on the right when you select the entry of business hours.

    Note that you cannot delete an entry of business hours if the entry contains appointments in the future.

    You can only delete an entry that either does not contain any future appointments or contains appointments in the past.

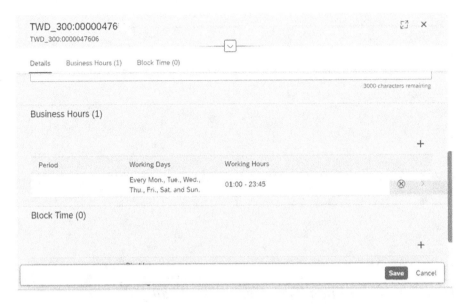

Figure 3-34. *Location Fiori screen (time details)*

- Modifying Business Hours

Figure 3-35. *Location Fiori screen (time details)*

Modifying Periods

You can increase or reduce the period. You can only reduce a period that does not contain any future appointments or contains appointments that are in the past. You cannot reduce the period, if the period that you are reducing contains appointments that are in the future.

Modifying Working Days

You can add a working day for the selected entry of business hours. Note that the system allows you to delete a working day for a time period only when the deleted working day does not contain any future appointments.

Modifying Working Hours

When you modify the working hours, there might be inconsistencies in the start and end time of the time slots. Hence, it is recommended that you modify the working hours in multiples of the time slot duration. You cannot modify the working hours, if the selected entry of business hours contains appointments that are in the future.

- Block Time

Figure 3-36. *Location Fiori screen (time details)*

Description

Specify a description for the time block.

Disable Appointment Booking

Specify whether you want to disable appointment booking only for the carriers or for all.

If you select For All, both you and the carriers cannot book appointments during the blocked time.

If you select For Carriers, only the carriers cannot book an appointment during the blocked time. The blocked time will be available for you to book an appointment.

Capacity

In the drop-down menu, you can view the capacity that you have specified for this loading point. You can select a capacity that you want to block from the drop-down menu.

Start Date and Time

Specify the start date and time for the time block.

End Date and Time

Specify the end date and time for the time block.

Docking Location

1. Choose the Docking Location tab on the left pane.

2. Choose the Add Docking Location button.

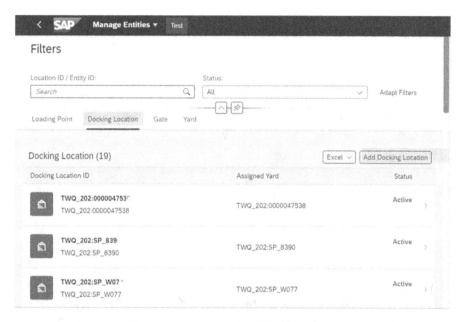

Figure 3-37. *Location Fiori screen (Add Docking Location)*

3. Define settings for the following sections:

   3.1. Details

      3.1.1. Location ID

            Select a location ID. You maintain location
            master data in the Manage Locations app.

Figure 3-38. *Location Fiori screen (Add Docking Location)*

3.1.2. Time Zone

Figure 3-39. *Location Fiori screen (Add Docking Location)*

3.1.3. Docking Location ID

Figure 3-40. *Location Fiori screen (Add Docking Location)*

3.1.4. Enable Cut-Off Time for Appointment Creation

You can choose whether you want to enable or disable the cut-off time for appointment creation for carriers. When you enable this setting, the system displays the Cut-Off Days and Time fields. You can enter the number of days and time before which all loading points at this docking location must stop accepting dock appointments from carriers. Note that the cut-off time is not applicable for warehouse operators.

Figure 3-41. Location Fiori screen (Add Docking Location)

3.1.5. Enable Appointment Date Change

If you enable the Enable Appointment Date Change indicator, the carriers can change the date of a dock appointment.

Figure 3-42. Location Fiori screen (Add Docking Location)

3.1.6.   Remarks

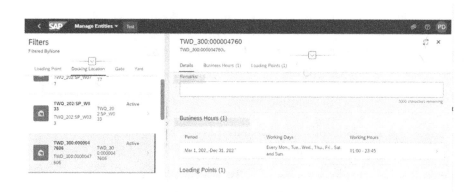

Figure 3-43. *Location Fiori screen*

3.2. Business Hours

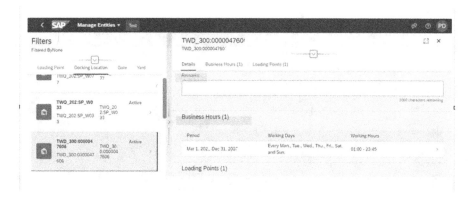

Figure 3-44. *Location Fiori screen*

Period

Specify the duration for which the entry of business hours is valid.

Working Days

Specify the working days of the docking location.

Working Hours

Specify the working hours for the specified working days.

3.3.   Loading Points

Choose the add icon in this section to add a loading point to the docking location. The system displays the list of active loading points in the same time zone that you have maintained in the Manage Entities app. You can select the loading points that you want to add to the docking location.

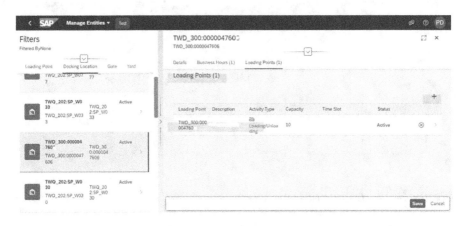

Figure 3-45. *Location Fiori screen (Add Docking Location)*

Gate

1. Choose the Gate tab on the left pane.

2. Choose the Add Gate button.

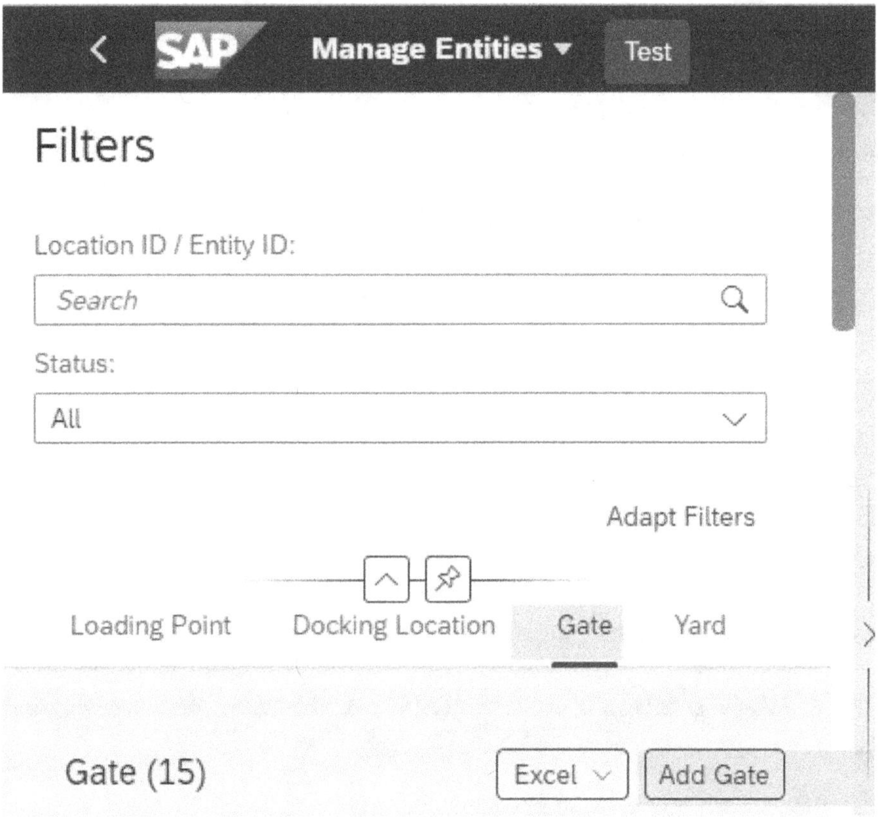

Figure 3-46. *Location Fiori screen (Add Gate)*

3. Define settings for the following sections

    3.1. Details

        3.1.1. Location ID

            Select a location ID. You maintain
            location master data in the Manage
            Locations app.

Figure 3-47. *Location Fiori screen (Add Gate)*

Time Zone

Enter a time zone.

3.1.2. Gate ID

Figure 3-48. *Location Fiori screen (Add Gate)*

3.1.3. Arrival Lead Time

Select the minimum time before which the driver must arrive at the gate.

Figure 3-49. *Location Fiori screen (Add Gate)*

3.1.4. Contact Name

Specify the name of a contact person responsible for this gate.

3.1.5. Phone Number

Specify the phone number of the contact person responsible for this gate.

3.1.6. Direction

Specify whether this gate supports inbound, outbound, or both inbound and outbound activities.

Figure 3-50. *Location Fiori screen (Add Gate)*

3.1.7. Enable Sharing with Yards

If you enable this setting, the gate can be associated with multiple yards in the same time zone. If you disable this setting, the gate can be associated with only one yard in the same time zone. When you enable this setting, the system displays the following:

Figure 3-51. *Location Fiori screen (Add Gate)*

3.1.8. Remarks

Enter the additional information about the gate.

3.2. Business Hours

Period

Specify the duration for which the entry of business hours is valid.

Working Days

Specify the working days of the gate.

Working Hours

Specify the working hours for the specified working days.

Figure 3-52. *Location Fiori screen (Add Gate)*

Yard

1. Choose the Yard tab on the left pane.

2. Choose the Add Yard button.

Figure 3-53. *Location Fiori screen (Add Yard)*

3.   Define settings for the following sections:

3.1. Details

3.1.1. Location ID

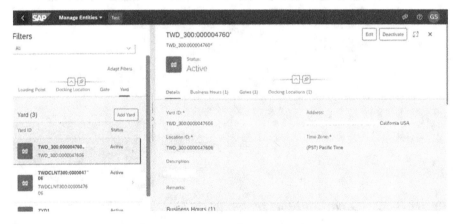

Figure 3-54. *Location Fiori screen (Add Yard)*

3.1.2. Time Zone

Enter a time zone.

3.1.3. Yard ID

Figure 3-55. *Location Fiori screen (Add Yard)*

3.1.4. Remarks

You can enter the additional information about the yard in this section.

3.2. Business Hours

Period

Specify the duration for which the entry of business hours is valid.

Working Days

Specify the working days of the yard.

Working Hours

Specify the working hours for the specified working days.

Figure 3-56. *Location Fiori screen (Add Yard)*

3.3. Gates

Choose the add icon in this section to add
entries of gates. The system displays the list of
active gates in the same time zone that you have
maintained in the Manage Entities app. You can
select the gates that you want to add to the yard.

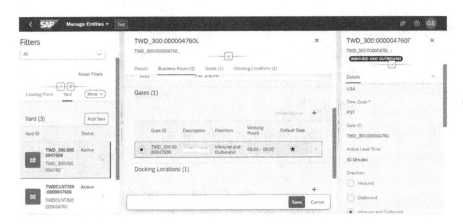

Figure 3-57. *Location Fiori screen (Add Yard)*

3.4. Docking Locations

Choose the add icon in this section to add
entries of docking locations. The system
displays the list of active docking locations in
the same time zone that you have maintained
in the Manage Entities app. You can select
the docking locations that you want to add to
the yard.

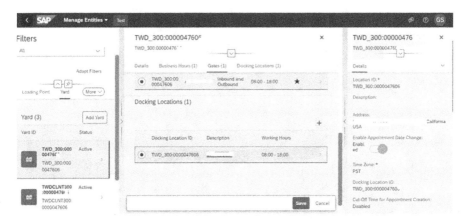

Figure 3-58. *Location Fiori screen (Add Yard)*

Summary

The **Create a Location** feature in SAP BN4L allows users to define and
add new locations essential for various logistics operations. By using this
feature, you can input key location details such as Location ID, Object
Type, Description, Country/Region, State, and City. This process helps
ensure accurate mapping of logistics activities to real-world geographic
locations, improving operational efficiency.

To create a location, users will access the **Manage Locations** screen from the **Master Data** section, click the **Create Location** button, and then enter the necessary location details. After entering the required information, the location is saved in the system. This feature is crucial for managing locations that impact freight orders, dock appointments, and other logistics processes.

CHAPTER 4

Configuring SAP BN4L

SAP BN4L, previously known as **Logistics Business Network (LBN)**, is a cloud-based platform that enhances logistics operations by offering real-time collaboration, seamless integration, and visibility across the entire supply chain. It connects various stakeholders, such as suppliers, customers, freight carriers, and logistics service providers, and enables businesses to optimize their logistics processes, track shipments in real time, and make informed decisions based on data-driven insights.

Configuring **SAP BN4L** is an essential step in leveraging its full potential, ensuring that it is tailored to the specific needs and structure of the organization. The configuration process involves several steps that allow businesses to set up their logistics networks, integrate with internal and external systems, and define the business rules that govern their logistics operations. Below is an overview of the key configuration details for **SAP BN4L.**

© Prince Tyagi, Anevershika 2025
P. Tyagi and Anevershika, *Getting Started with BN4L and GTT Integrations for SAP*,
https://doi.org/10.1007/979-8-8688-1405-1_4

Key Components of SAP BN4L Configuration

1. **Initial Setup and System Integration:** The first step in configuring SAP BN4L is establishing the system's integration with existing ERP systems, such as **SAP S/4HANA** or **SAP ERP**, and other third-party solutions. This integration ensures that logistics-related data flows seamlessly between systems, eliminating silos and improving operational efficiency. SAP BN4L can be connected to various systems through APIs, web services, and pre-built integration packages. The integration setup involves configuring communication channels, defining interfaces, and mapping data between the systems.

2. **Define and Configure Logistics Network:** The logistics network is the backbone of SAP BN4L, consisting of various locations, stakeholders, and logistics partners. Configuring the network involves defining and managing these locations, such as warehouses, distribution centers, suppliers, and customer locations. Administrators can create, modify, or delete location data, ensuring that all relevant partners and facilities are included in the logistics ecosystem. In addition, the configuration process includes setting up transportation lanes, defining the logistics flow, and assigning transportation routes between various network nodes.

3. **User Management and Access Control:** Proper access control is critical in any logistics platform to ensure that sensitive business data is protected while enabling relevant stakeholders to access the necessary information. In SAP BN4L, administrators configure user roles, permissions, and access levels

based on business requirements. For example, the system allows the creation of roles for logistics managers, suppliers, carriers, and other stakeholders. Access control ensures that each user can only view or perform tasks relevant to their responsibilities, improving both security and efficiency.

4. **Partner Setup and Collaboration**: A significant strength of SAP BN4L is its ability to facilitate collaboration between different stakeholders. Configuring business partners such as suppliers, customers, freight carriers, and logistics service providers is a crucial part of the setup process. The configuration process involves defining partner profiles, including contact details, service-level agreements (SLAs), and other key business terms. Once partners are set up, businesses can start exchanging information in real time, such as shipment tracking, order fulfillment, and inventory updates, improving transparency and collaboration across the supply chain.

5. **Configure Freight and Transport Management**: Freight management is a core feature of SAP BN4L, enabling organizations to optimize their transportation operations. Configuring freight management involves defining transportation rates, establishing service levels, and creating rules for freight execution. The system also allows businesses to manage transportation bookings, track shipments, and handle freight settlements. In addition, SAP BN4L integrates with **SAP Transportation Management (SAP TM)** to ensure that transportation planning, execution, and monitoring are seamlessly connected to the logistics network.

6. **Set Up Real-Time Tracking and Monitoring**: One of the most powerful features of SAP BN4L is its ability to provide real-time visibility into the status of goods, shipments, and logistics operations. Configuration includes setting up tracking parameters, enabling sensor data (IoT integration), and defining tracking milestones for different types of shipments. Businesses can configure alerts and notifications to proactively manage delays, disruptions, and exceptions in the logistics process. The system also allows users to monitor shipment progress, receive alerts, and resolve potential issues in real time.

7. **Define Business Rules and Workflows**: SAP BN4L allows businesses to define specific rules and workflows that govern the logistics process. These rules can include shipment approval processes, routing guidelines, freight selection criteria, and other business logic necessary for effective logistics management. By configuring workflows and rules, organizations can automate various tasks, such as order processing, shipment planning, and inventory updates, leading to reduced manual effort and enhanced operational efficiency.

8. **Performance Analytics and Reporting Setup**: Another critical aspect of the configuration is setting up analytics and reporting features. SAP BN4L offers robust reporting capabilities, enabling businesses to gain insights into key performance indicators (KPIs) such as on-time deliveries, freight costs, inventory levels, and supplier performance.

Configuring analytics involves defining the metrics that are most important to the business, setting up dashboards, and creating reports that are accessible to stakeholders. These insights help organizations monitor performance, identify trends, and make data-driven decisions to optimize their logistics operations.

This section walks through the BN4L and GTT basis configuration settings, offering a comprehensive guide to help you seamlessly access and operate the applications. The steps outlined in this section ensure that you can configure the systems correctly while understanding how to use the full range of features provided by BN4L and GTT. Detailed, sequential instructions are presented to help you perform each setup task effectively, reducing the risk of configuration errors. By following this process, users are set up for streamlined workflows and consistent performance. Overall, this section lays a solid foundation for establishing efficient and reliable operations across your logistics and tracking environments.

Concepts and Terms

- BN4L—Business Network for Logistics
- Purchasing organization
- LBN ID

The following setup needs to be done in Shipper Tenant, Carrier Tenant, and the SAP TM back-end system in three simple steps.
To ensure successful collaboration and data exchange between shipper and carrier environments, the configuration must be carried out across three key areas: the shipper's tenant, the carrier's tenant, and the SAP Transportation Management (TM) back-end system. These steps form the core foundation for enabling end-to-end freight collaboration functionality:

- Step 1: Linking Shipper LBN ID with the Carrier LBN ID (by discovering the carrier in Shipper Tenant)

- Step 2: Assigning Carrier LBN ID to Carrier Business Partner (BP) in SAP TM system

- Step 3: Assigning Shipper LBN ID to the BP of the Purchase Organization in SAP TM system

Step 1: Linking Shipper LBN ID with the Carrier LBN ID (by discovering the carrier in Shipper Tenant)

To begin the setup, identify the specific Carrier LBN ID that should be connected with the respective Shipper LBN ID. After identifying the carrier, access the Carrier Tenant using the credentials linked to that LBN ID. This is the initial login step that establishes the foundation for subsequent discovery and linking. Refer to Figure 4-1 for a visual representation of logging in to the relevant Carrier Tenant associated with the chosen LBN ID.

Figure 4-1. *Log in to the Carrier Tenant of the LBN ID*

Navigate to the **Manage Business Profile** section within the Carrier Tenant, and activate the following critical options:

- **Make the Business Profile Visible to Potential Business Partners**: This step is essential as it allows the Shipper Tenant to detect and identify the carrier during the discovery process. Without enabling this, the carrier will not be discoverable in the shipper's network.

- **Automatically Accept Connection Requests
  (Invitations)**: Enabling this option allows automatic
  acceptance of connection invitations from the shipper.
  If the shipper sends a request to connect with the
  carrier, the system will auto-approve it without any
  manual action. However, if this option is not enabled,
  the carrier can still manually review and approve the
  invitation. Refer to Figure 4-2 for an example showing
  the activation of this option in the carrier's tenant
  under the business profile settings.

Figure 4-2. *Enable the Business Partner in the Carrier Tenant in
Manage Business Profile tiles*

Select the **Shipper Tenant** associated with the specific **Shipper LBN
ID**, and then navigate to the **Discover Business Partners** tab. Within this
section, search for and locate the **Carrier LBN ID** that needs to be linked
with the shipper. This functionality enables the shipper to identify and
initiate a connection with the correct carrier in order to establish seamless
collaboration through the network.

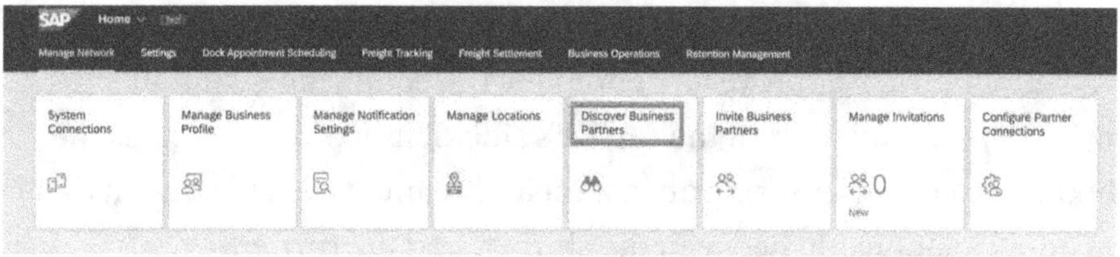

Figure 4-3. *Discover Business Partners in Shipper Tenant*

Searching the Carrier LBN ID in the Shipper Tenant

When attempting to search for the **Carrier LBN ID** within the **Shipper Tenant**, ensure that the carrier's **Business Profile** has been activated. If this profile is not enabled on the carrier's end, the corresponding **Carrier LBN ID** will not appear or be visible in the Shipper Tenant during the discovery process. Activation of the business profile is a prerequisite for successful visibility and connection.

Figure 4-4. *Searching Carrier LBN ID in Shipper Tenant*

Click the "Request for connection" tab for accepting the carrier in Shipper Tenant, and since the "Automatically accept connection requests" setting is enabled in Carrier Tenant, automatically the connection will be established.

To initiate the connection with the carrier from within the **Shipper Tenant**, select the **Request for connection"** tab. This action sends a connection request to the carrier. If the Carrier Tenant has the **"Automatically accept connection requests"** setting activated, the system will automatically approve and complete the connection without any manual intervention from the carrier's side. This feature simplifies the linking process by ensuring an instant and seamless establishment of the business relationship between the shipper and the carrier.

Figure 4-5. *Carrier LBN ID connected to the Shipper LBN ID*

Step 2: Assigning Carrier LBN ID to Carrier Business Partner(BP) in SAP TM System

Prior to linking the Carrier LBN ID with the respective Carrier Business Partner (BP) in the SAP TM system, it is essential to first configure an EDI communication profile tailored for freight-order-related settings.

To carry out this configuration, navigate through the following path in the system:

IMG ➤ Transportation Management ➤ Integration ➤ Enterprise Services ➤ Define EDI Communication Profile, as illustrated in Figure 4-6.

127

Figure 4-6. *Path to access "Define EDI Communication Profile"*

In EDI Communication Profile, we need to set the following:

- **Send EDI Notification Messages**: When this check box is activated, the system utilizes the service interface **TransportationOrderRequest_Out** to transmit notification messages reflecting any late-stage modifications. This ensures timely communication of changes to the relevant recipients.

- **Include Charge in EDI Message**: Enabling this check box ensures that cost-related components are incorporated within the message sent through the interface **TransportationOrderRequest_Out**, thereby delivering complete Freight Order information, inclusive of pricing.

- **Send Tracking Relevance Indicator**: This option
  is used to communicate a request from the shipper,
  instructing the carrier to provide tracking data on
  transportation events, such as when a shipment
  leaves a distribution center or reaches the customer's
  location. Activating this setting allows the tracking
  relevance indicator to be passed through the interface
  TransportationOrderRequest_Out. Refer to **Figure 4-7**
  to review the configuration setup.

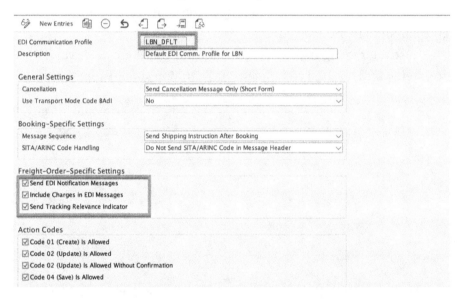

Figure 4-7. *Setting freight-order-specific settings in EDI*
Communication Profile

**Assign EDI Communication Profile and the Carrier LBN ID for the
Carrier BP in S/4 HANA TM system using the Transaction Code BP.**
To configure the carrier in the SAP S/4HANA TM back end, start by
launching **Transaction Code BP**. Within the Business Partner interface,
ensure that the **BP Role** is set to **Carrier (CRM010)**. Once selected,
navigate to the **Identification** tab.

Within this section, under the **Transportation Management** area, assign the appropriate **EDI Communication Profile** that has already been created to handle freight-order-specific communication settings. This step ensures that messages such as shipment updates and notifications can be exchanged effectively with external carriers.

Following that, locate the **Identification Numbers** section, and input the **Carrier LBN ID**. This ID must be entered under the **ID type LBN001**, which is the designated type for Business Network Logistics identifiers. This configuration step is crucial for establishing a correct mapping between the carrier's identity in the logistics network and its representation in the TM system.

Please refer to **Figure 4-8** for a visual guide on where these values are entered and how the completed configuration should appear within the system.

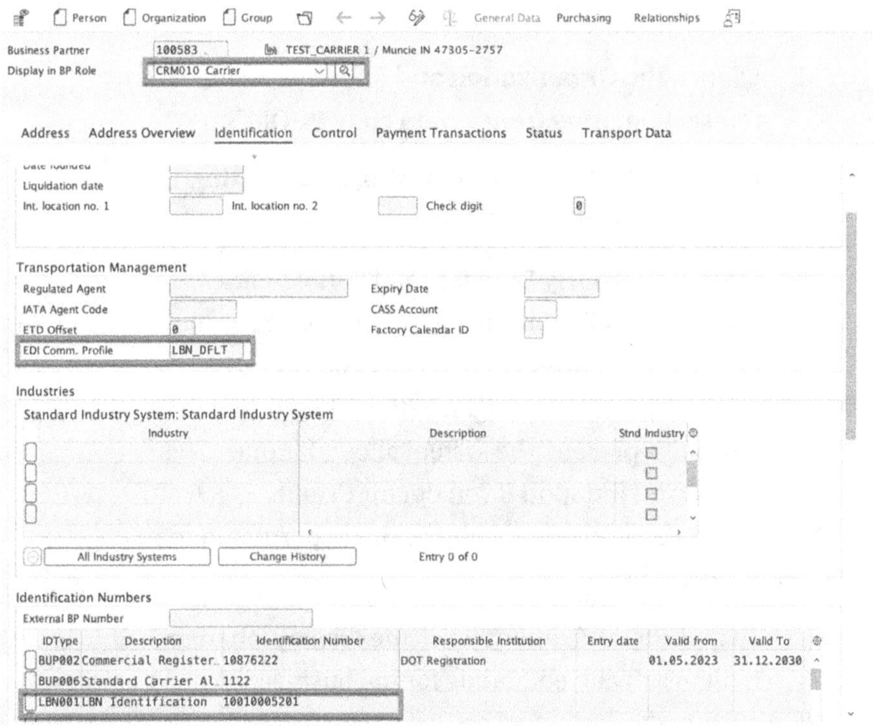

Figure 4-8. *EDI Communication Profile and the Carrier LBN ID assigned to the Carrier BP in S/4 HANA TM system*

Step 3: Assigning Shipper LBN ID to the BP of the Purchase Organization in SAP TM System

For correct system behavior within the logistics network, it's essential that the **Shipper LBN ID** is accurately updated and maintained. Each purchasing organization receives a unique **LBN ID** from **SAP BN4L Freight Collaboration**, which serves as the official identifier used during business process exchanges across the logistics network. You can retrieve this identifier by navigating to the **Manage Business Profile** application within your SAP system. To ensure smooth integration with the Transportation Management solution, the following process must be followed for updating this LBN ID:

Procedure:

1. Launch the **Organization and Staffing Change** transaction using **transaction code PPOME.**

2. Locate and select the **purchasing organization ID** that requires the LBN ID update.

3. Switch to the **Org. Data** tab, and double-click the **Business Partner** field. This action will open the business partner view associated with the selected purchasing organization. If no business partner is present, the system allows for one to be created on the spot. If you opt for **Create**, SAP will automatically generate the business partner in the background.

4. To make modifications, click the **display/change icon** to activate edit mode for the business partner data.

5. Proceed to the **Identification** tab. In the **Identification Numbers** section, enter **LBN001** into the **IDType** field.

6. Fill in the **LBN ID** in the corresponding **Identification Number** field, and commit your changes by saving.

Next, identify the **Purchase Organization** tied to the specific **Freight Order (FO)** scenario. Use **T.code PPOME** within your **S/4 HANA TM** system to access the Purchase Organization. Then, under the **Organization Data** tab, record the **Business Partner Number** assigned to it, as illustrated in **Figure 4-9.**

Figure 4-9. *Identifying the Business Partner for the given Purchase Organization*

Open the **Business Partner** that was retrieved from the **Purchase Organization** within the **T.code BP** in the **S/4 HANA TM** system, and assign the appropriate **BP role** as **General (000000)**. Then, proceed to the **Identification Numbers** section, and enter the **Shipper LBN ID** in the **ID type LBN001** field, as demonstrated in **Figure 4-10**.

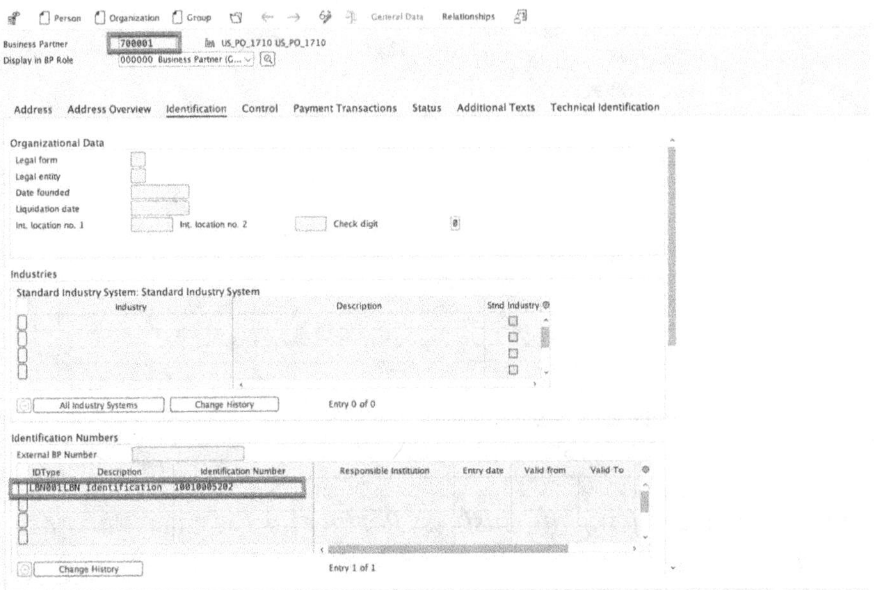

Figure 4-10. *Assigning the Shipper LBN ID to the Business Partner of the respective Purchase Organization used in Freight Order*

Once all the settings are complete, including the linking of the **Carrier LBN ID**, **Shipper LBN ID**, and the **Business Partner** within the **S/4 HANA TM** system, it will be possible to execute all the various scenarios that fall under the scope of **Freight Collaboration**.

Define Identification Types

System	TM System XX**
Component/Module	TM
Customizing Path	SPRO ➤ Cross Application Components ➤ SAP Business Partner ➤ Business Partner ➤ Basic Settings ➤ Identification Numbers ➤ Define Identification Types
Customizing Transaction	N/A
Cross Client Object	No
Transportable Object	Yes

Settings:

- New Entry : LBN001

Rationale:

- To define the identification type to be used for integration with BN4L. This identification type will capture the LBN ID of the carrier.

Define Identification Categories

System	SAP TM
Component/Module	SAP TM
Customizing Path	SPRO ➤ Cross Application Components ➤ SAP Business Partner ➤ Business Partner ➤ Basic Settings ➤ Identification Numbers ➤ Define Identification Categories

Settings:

- Identification category: LBN001

  Linking of identification type LBN001 to Business
  Partner. This is required to have system maintain LBN ID
  at the business partner level and connection to BN4L.

Define EDI Communication Profile

Component/Module	TM
Customizing Path	SPRO ➤ SAP Transportation Management ➤ Integration ➤ Enterprise Services ➤ Define EDI Communication Profile

Settings:

- **LBN_DFLT**

  EDI Communication Profile contains settings for the
  communication with the carrier, for example, the
  message sequence and if cancellations are to be sent
  with or without content. This profile is assigned to the
  carrier in business partner master data (Carrier role,
  Vendor Data tab page).

Maintain Text Schema

Component/Module	TM
Customizing Path	SPRO ➤ Cross Application Components ➤ Reusable Objects and Functions for BOPF Environment ➤ Dependent Object Text Collection ➤ Maintain Text Schema

Settings:

- BN4L Note New Text Type: E0103

  Text type E0103 is used for receiving NOTES entered by carrier in BN4L Freight Collaboration. This text type is predefined in the Transportation order confirmation In message.

Assign Text Code

System	BN4L Shipper Tenant
Component/Module	BN4L Freight Collaboration
Customizing Path	FIORI App—"Assign Codes"

Settings:

- In Shipper Tenant, navigate to Assign Codes App.
- From the code list, select the option Note Type.
  - Code in external system: E0102
  - LBN Code: RMARK (Remarks)

As a shipper, if there are any instructions that need to be shared with carrier along with the transportation order request. The text type used in TM9.6 for this E0102. This text type is mapped with LBN text type—RMARK.

Maintain Ordering Party in LBN

Navigate to "General Settings" Fiori tile in Shipper Tenant. The General Settings app enables you as the shipper admin to configure the general settings related to freight collaboration at an ordering party level.

Note that to add an ordering party, you must have already created a location in the Manage Locations app with the Object Type as Business Partner.

Figure 4-11. General settings

Select add ordering party.

Figure 4-12. General settings

A pop-up would appear; select the ordering party you wish to maintain.

Figure 4-13. General settings

The selected party would then appear as ordering party.

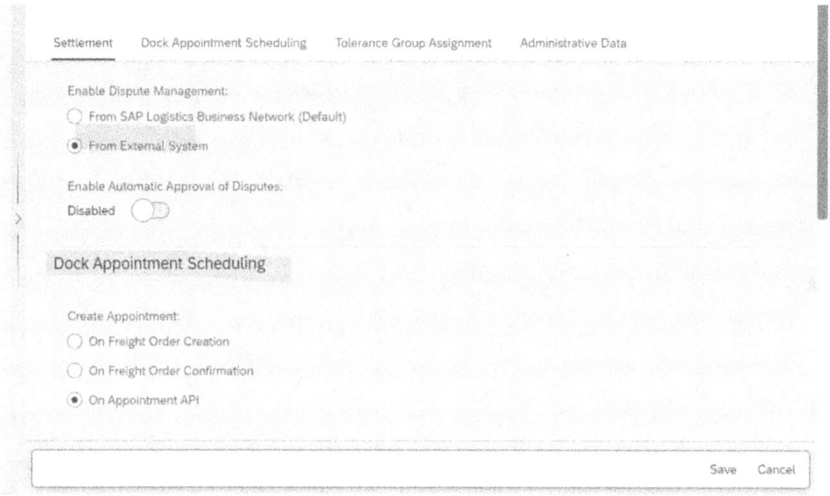

Figure 4-14. *General settings*

Summary

Configuring SAP BN4L is a comprehensive and multistep process that requires careful planning, integration, and execution. By successfully configuring the platform, businesses can unlock its full potential to enhance logistics operations, streamline collaboration, and gain real-time visibility into their supply chain activities. With the proper configuration, SAP BN4L enables businesses to optimize transportation management, track shipments, monitor performance, and improve decision-making all while ensuring the security and compliance of logistics processes.

This chapter serves as an overview of the key configuration details, but the true power of SAP BN4L lies in its ability to integrate and automate complex logistics operations, delivering improved efficiency and agility in a competitive global marketplace.

CHAPTER 5

Configuring SAP GTT

In today's complex and interconnected supply chain environment, real-time visibility and traceability of goods and shipments are paramount for operational efficiency and customer satisfaction. **SAP Global Track and Trace (GTT)** provides businesses with a powerful tool to track the movement and status of goods across the entire supply chain. Through **GTT**, businesses can gain end-to-end visibility, reduce delays, ensure compliance, and make data-driven decisions that enhance the overall supply chain experience.

However, in order to fully realize the benefits of **SAP GTT**, careful and detailed configuration is required. This chapter delves into the configuration process for **SAP Global Track and Trace (GTT)**, highlighting the key steps and components involved in setting up GTT within the SAP ecosystem. The configuration of GTT ensures that all stakeholders involved in the supply chain—ranging from suppliers and manufacturers to logistics providers and customers—can track, trace, and manage shipments with precision and efficiency.

Overview of SAP GTT Configuration

The **SAP Global Track and Trace (GTT)** solution provides end-to-end visibility into logistics processes by tracking goods across various points in the supply chain. GTT integrates with various other SAP solutions, such as **SAP S/4HANA, SAP BN4L, SAP Transportation Management (TM)**, and **SAP Event Management (EM)** to provide real-time insights into the status of shipments, containers, inventory, and other critical supply chain elements.

© Prince Tyagi, Anevershika 2025
P. Tyagi and Anevershika, *Getting Started with BN4L and GTT Integrations for SAP*,
https://doi.org/10.1007/979-8-8688-1405-1_5

Configuring **SAP GTT** involves several essential tasks that ensure the system is integrated with other SAP systems, able to track and trace goods efficiently, and aligned with business processes. The goal of this configuration is to ensure that all necessary tracking and monitoring data is collected, processed, and presented to the user in a way that is actionable and insightful.

Key Components of GTT Configuration

1. **System Integration and Data Exchange Setup**: The first step in configuring **SAP GTT** is establishing robust integration with other systems in the SAP ecosystem. GTT needs to interact with various SAP modules, including **SAP TM** for transportation management, **SAP S/4HANA** for inventory and order management, and **SAP Event Management** for event tracking.

   - **Integration with SAP TM**: Configure integration points for monitoring transportation orders, tracking freight movements, and ensuring that shipment milestones are recorded.

   - **Integration with SAP S/4HANA**: Ensure the synchronization of inventory and goods movement data, so that SAP GTT can provide real-time visibility into stock levels, shipping statuses, and order fulfillment.

2. **Defining Tracking Objects**: Tracking objects are essential elements that SAP GTT tracks throughout the logistics process. These objects could include shipments, orders, containers, or even individual products. Properly defining and categorizing these tracking objects is critical to ensuring that all necessary data points are collected.

- **Shipment Tracking**: Define the types of shipments you want to track, whether they are full truckloads (FTL), less-than-truckloads (LTL), air freight, ocean freight, or parcel shipments.

- **Container and Package Tracking**: Configure container and package types, including identifiers such as shipping labels or tracking numbers. This setup ensures that goods are traced accurately at every stage of transport.

- **Product and Inventory Tracking**: Track products and inventory by linking tracking objects with materials or products. This configuration ensures visibility into the quantity, location, and status of products at all times.

3. **Defining Events and Milestones**: GTT relies on tracking key events and milestones that occur during the shipment process. These events are critical to providing end-to-end visibility. Examples of milestones include

    - Goods departure from the warehouse

    - In-transit status updates (e.g., customs clearance, crossing borders)

    - Estimated time of arrival (ETA) at the destination

    - Delays or disruptions in transit

    - Goods arrival and delivery confirmation

Configuring events and milestones involves setting up the various stages that a shipment will go through in the supply chain. GTT tracks these milestones and provides updates, alerting stakeholders if delays or exceptions occur. Event definitions and workflows need to be established within **SAP Event Management (EM)** to capture these events and ensure they are processed in real time.

4. **Defining Track and Trace Parameters**: SAP GTT allows businesses to configure traceability parameters to determine how the system should collect and process tracking data. This configuration includes defining the following elements:

   - **Tracking Frequencies**: Specify how frequently updates and statuses should be collected from stakeholders, such as transportation providers, suppliers, or customers.

   - **Data Sources**: Identify where tracking data is coming from—whether from GPS sensors, RFID tags, barcodes, or partner systems. You will need to configure data sources for tracking shipments based on the data capture mechanisms available to you.

   - **Data Collection Methods**: Define whether the system will collect event data via manual entry, automated sensors, or integration with external tracking systems like **Telematics** or **IoT-enabled devices**.

5. **Defining Exception Management Rules**:

    Exception management is a critical aspect of SAP GTT configuration. When tracking shipments, unexpected events such as delays, customs hold-ups, or missed delivery windows are inevitable. SAP GTT allows users to define exception rules to identify and handle such occurrences. For example:

    - **Delay Alerts**: Define threshold limits for acceptable delivery times. If a shipment exceeds this threshold, an exception will be triggered, and relevant parties will be notified.

    - **Damage or Loss Reporting**: In the event of a damaged or lost shipment, the system should automatically raise an exception and prompt stakeholders to take action.

    - **Route Deviations**: If a shipment deviates from the planned route, an alert is generated, allowing for corrective actions.

These exceptions need to be configured to trigger automatic workflows, such as notifying the logistics team, creating an incident report, or adjusting delivery schedules.

Key Business Rules

BN4L GTT will be used for order tracking, and events available in GTT will be send to the TM freight order.

BN4L Global Track and Trace (GTT) tenant is connected to the SAP ERP system. Both systems are connected via direct connection with BN4L GTT.

Configuration on SAPS4 HANA

BTE Configuration

To activate the application interface for process and event tracking in the SAP S/4HANA system, we have set the PI-EM indicator in BF11.

System	SAP ERP
Component/Module	BN4L GTT
Customizing Transaction	BF11

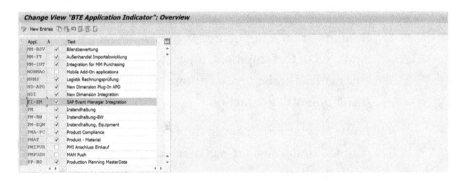

Figure 5-1. BTE configuration

Download ABAP Code

System	SAP ERP
Component/Module	BN4L GTT

Report: ABAP Git link https://docs.abapgit.org/user-guide/getting-started/install.html

GTT objects are downloaded as zip file from https://github.com/SAP-samples/logistics-business-network-gtt-standardapps-samples.git.

Report: ABAPGIT_STANDALONE needs to execute in offline mode with all the provided standard packages. And make sure all the objects are successfully activated.

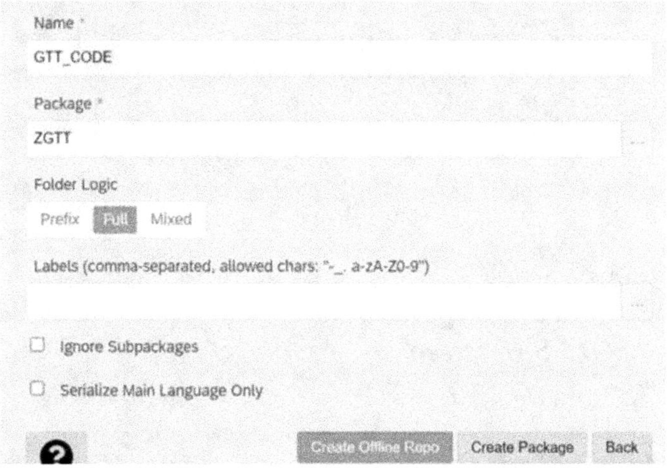

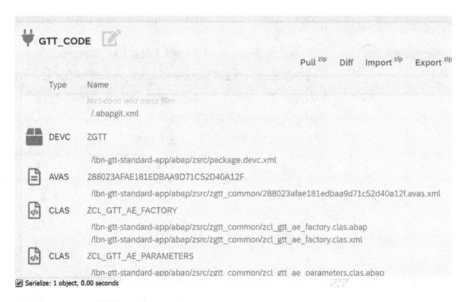

Figure 5-2. Execution screen

Figure 5-3. GTT code activation

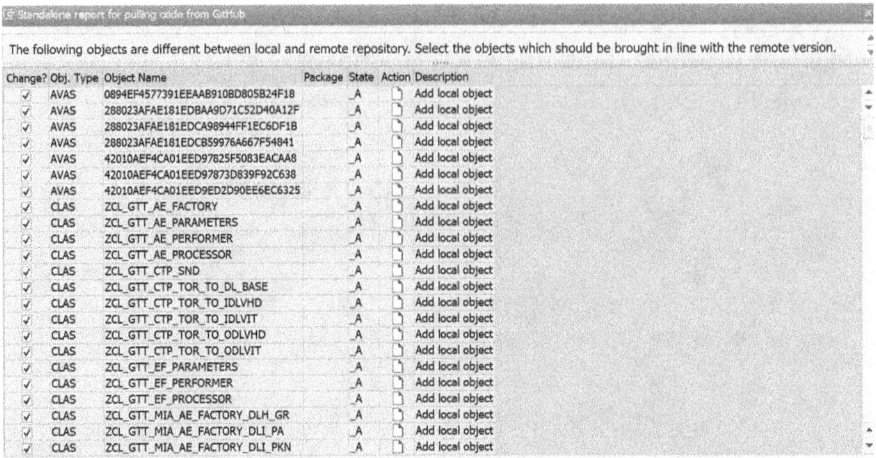

Figure 5-4. GTT SAP screen

Import BC Set

System	SAP ERP
Component/Module	BN4L GTT
Customizing Path	Display IMG ➤ Integration with Other SAP Components ➤ Interface to Global Track and Trace ➤ Define Application Interface ➤ Define Used Business Process Types, Appl. Object Types and Event Types ➤ Define Used Business Process Types

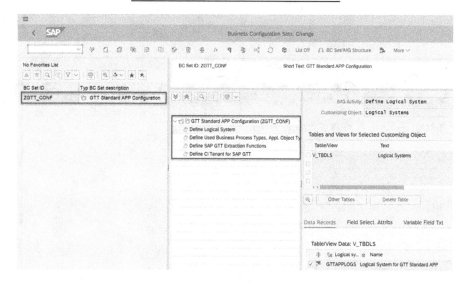

Figure 5-5. *BC sets activation*

Business Process Types for sales order (ESC_SORDER), purchase order (ESC_PORDER), and (ESC_DELIV) are maintained as "Active."

BC was downloaded locally in .bcs file extension and uploaded via SCPR3.

System	SAP ERP
Component/Module	BN4L GTT
Tcode	SCPR3

Figure 5-6. *BC sets activation*

149

Activate the BC set from the SAP Easy Access Menu, Tools ➤ Customizing ➤ Business Configuration Sets ➤ Activation of BC Sets (Transaction Code SCPR20). The following message is displayed:

"Caution You have started the BC Set activation If you continue, new data records will be created and/or existing ones overwritten."

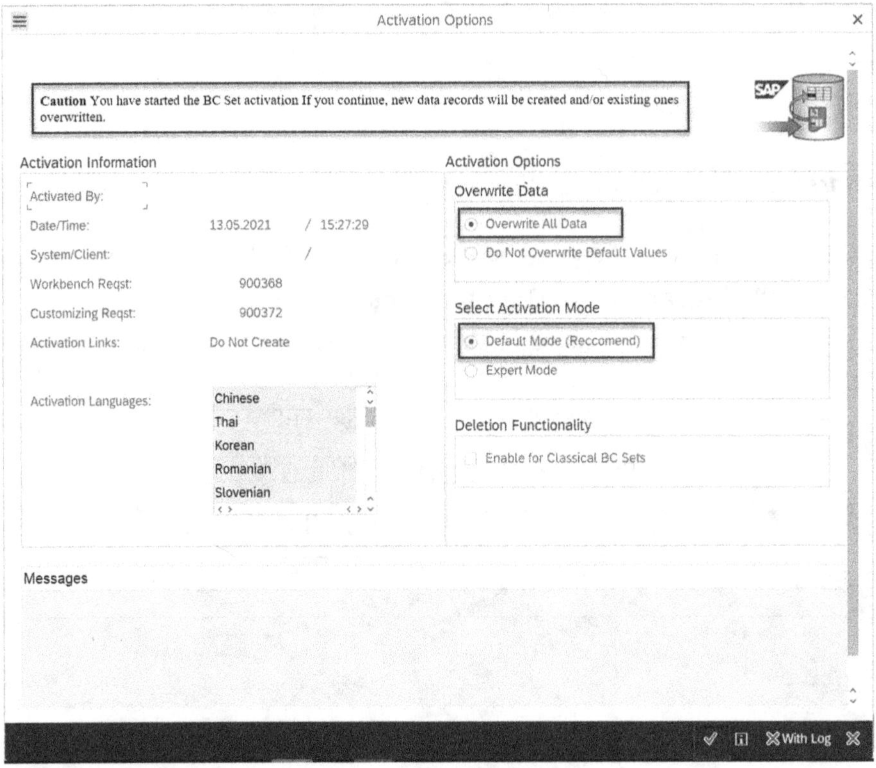

Figure 5-7. BC sets activation

Below are **Activation Logs** after the activation was done.

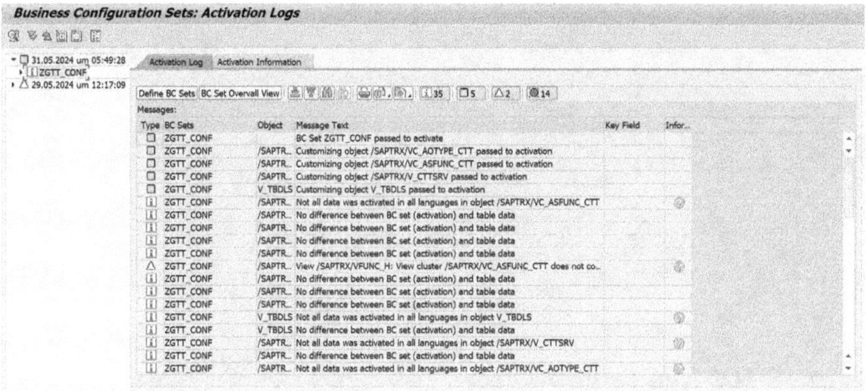

Figure 5-8. *BC sets activation*

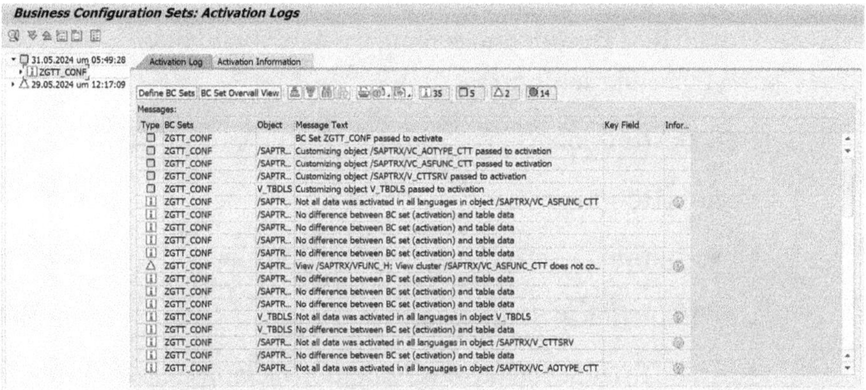

Figure 5-9. *BC sets activation*

Define RFC Connection for SAP BN4L GTT

System	SAP ERP
Component/Module	BN4L GTT
Tcode	SM59

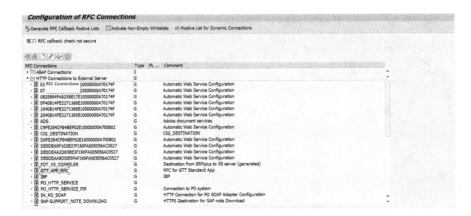

Figure 5-10. RFC connection

Documents from S4 HANA will be sent to BN4L GTT via IDOCs. Hence, this object GTT_APP_RFC needs to be created with the below settings:

- On the RFC Destination screen, we have maintained the following settings:

    RFC Destination: GTT_APP_RFC

    Connection Type: G

    Description: Description for this RFC destination

    On the Technical Settings tab:

    Host: bn4l-i9u3ce9p.gtt-flp-lbnplatform.cfapps.eu10. hana.ondemand.com

    Port: 443

    Path Prefix: /api/idoc/em/v1/ TrackedProcessAndEvent

    (To send IDOC GTTMSG01 from S4 to BN4L GTT)

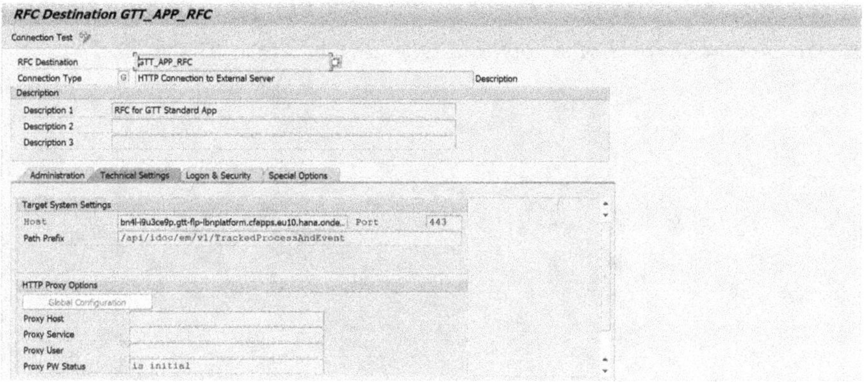

Figure 5-11. *RFC connection setup*

- On the Login & Security tab:

  Logon Procedure

  Logon with User: Basic Authentication with the
  technical user credentials is maintained. This technical
  user is also registered in SAP BN4L Global Track and
  Trace subaccount on the SAP BTP.

  Logon with Ticket: Default value Do Not Send
  Logon Ticket.

  Status of Secure Protocol: Active in SSL.

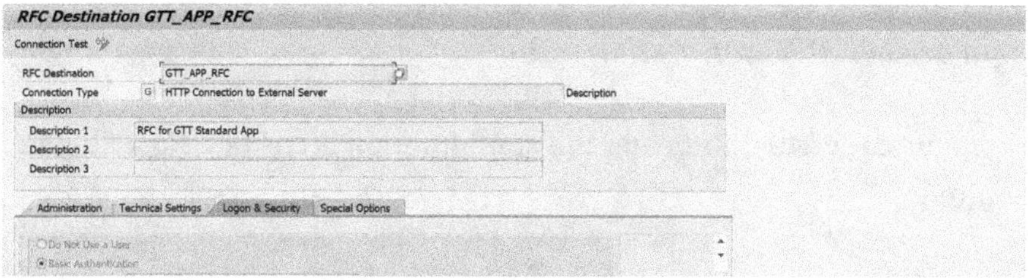

Figure 5-12. *RFC connection setup*

It is advised to change the user email in the RFC to a separate technical user account which is not associated with any business user later.

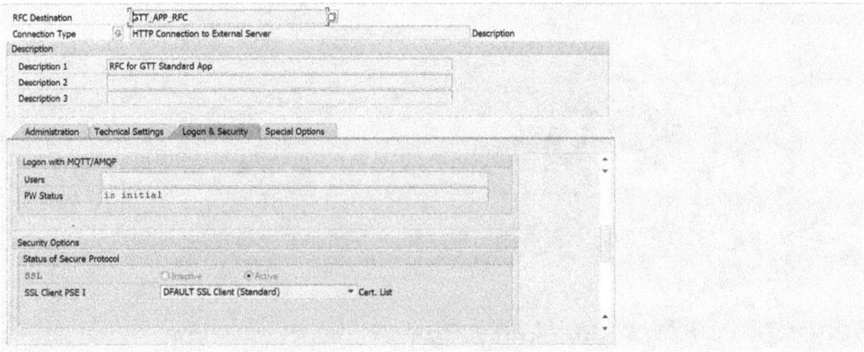

Figure 5-13. *RFC connection setup*

Figure 5-14. *RFC connection setup*

Status code "403" indicates the configuration is correct. No action is required.

Define Ports (Manual Activity Not TR)

System	SAP ERP
Component/Module	BN4L GTT
SPRO Path	**Display IMG** page, click **Integration with Other SAP Components ➤ Interface to Global Track and Trace ➤ IDoc Settings.** Choose activity **Define Ports.**

In XML HTTP folder, a new port GTTAPPPORT has to be created with the following details:

RFC Destination: GTT_APP_RFC.

Content Type: application/x-sap.idoc.

HTTP Version: Version 1.0. SOAP Protocol is checked.

Figure 5-15. *Port setup*

Define Partner Profiles (Manual Activity Not TR)

System	SAP ERP
Component/Module	BN4L GTT
SPRO Path	In **Display IMG** page, unfold **Integration with Other SAP Components ➤ Interface to Global Track and Trace ➤ IDoc Settings.** Choose activity **Define Partner Profiles**

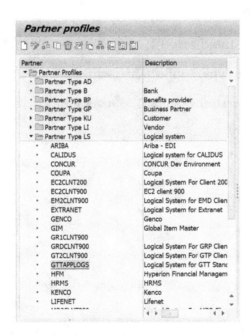

Figure 5-16. *Partner profile*

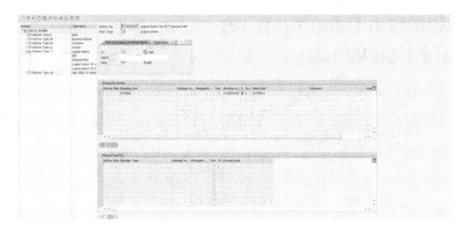

Figure 5-17. *Partner profile*

Under the **Outbound** box, a new outbound parameter is maintained.

In the **Message Type,** added GTTMSG and Receiver Port GTTAPPPORT are maintained.

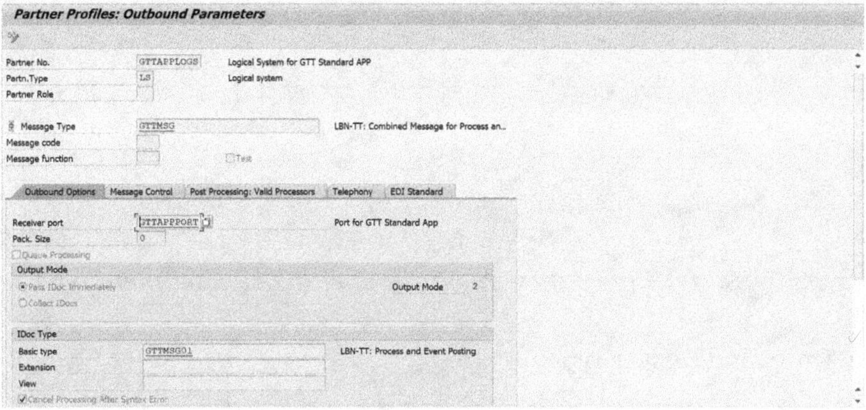

Figure 5-18. *Partner profile*

Maintain Document Types for GTT Relevancy

Document types relevant for GTT integration are maintained in the standard tables as follows and marked as "active":

Sales Order Type:

System	SAP ERP
Component/Module	BN4L GTT
Tcode	Z****GTT_SOTYPE_RST

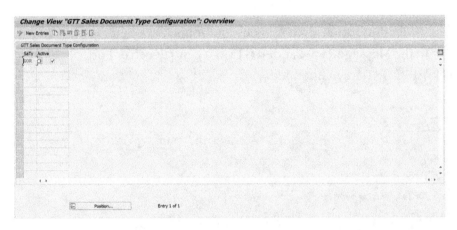

Figure 5-19. *GTT relevancy integration with SAP document type*

Outbound Deliver Type:

System	SAP ERP
Component/Module	BN4L GTT
Tcode	Z****GTT_DLVTYPE_RST

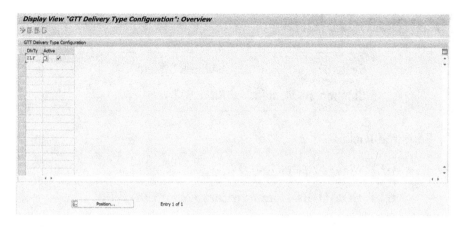

Figure 5-20. *GTT relevancy integration with SAP document type*

Stock Transfer Order Type:

System	SAP ERP
Component/Module	BN4L GTT
Tcode	Z***GTT_POTYPE_RST - GTT

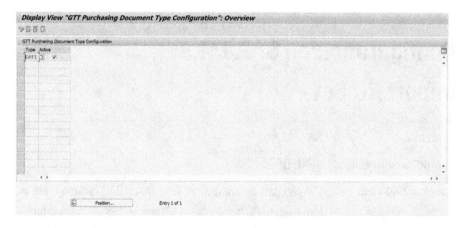

Figure 5-21. *GTT relevancy integration with SAP document type*

Technical Details

System	SAP ERP System XX**
Component/Module	BN4L GTT

Required Packages:

GTT: Main package for GTT

GTT_COMMON: Common package for LBN GTT integration

GTT_MIA: Monitoring inbound ASNs

GTT_POF: ABAP package for LBN GTT PO fulfillment APP

GTT_SOF: ABAP package for LBN GTT SO/OBD fulfillment APP

GTT_STS: Standard tracking shipment

Configuration on SAP TM
Import BC Set

System	SAP TM
Component/Module	BN4L GTT
Customizing Path	Display IMG ➤ Integration with Other SAP Components ➤ Interface to Global Track and Trace ➤ Define Application Interface ➤ Define Used Business Process Types, Appl. Object Types and Event Types ➤ Define Used Business Process Types

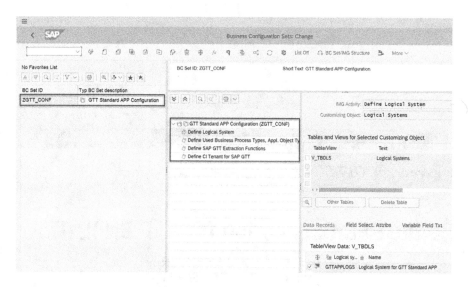

Figure 5-22. GTT Business Process Type

The Business Process Type TMS_TOR is maintained as Active by default.

BC set was downloaded in the local computer with a .bcs file extension.

System	SAP TM
Component/Module	BN4L GTT
Tcode	SCPR3

Figure 5-23. GTT BC set

Activate the BC set from the SAP Easy Access Menu, **Tools ➤ Customizing ➤ Business Configuration Sets ➤ Activation of BC Sets** (Transaction Code SCPR20). The following message is displayed:

"Caution You have started the BC Set activation If you continue, new data records will be created and/or existing ones overwritten."

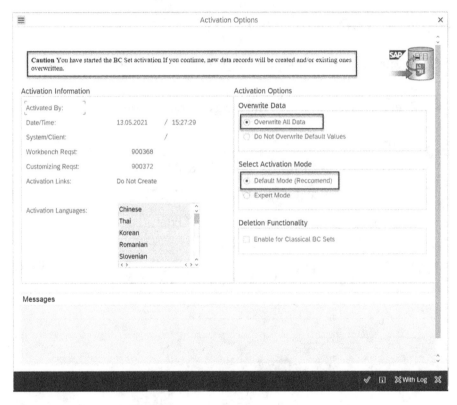

Figure 5-24. *GTT BC set*

Define RFC Connection for SAP BN4L GTT

System	SAP TM
Component/Module	BN4L GTT
Tcode	SM59

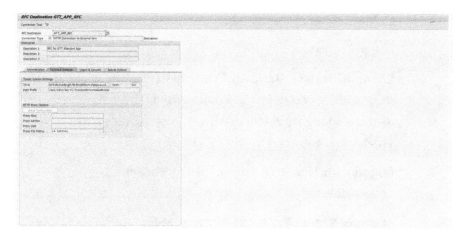

Figure 5-25. *GTT RFC destination*

Documents from TM will be sent to BN4L GTT via IDOCs. Hence, GTT_APP_RFC with the below settings:

- On the RFC Destination screen, we have maintained the following settings:

  RFC Destination: GTT_APP_RFC

  Connection Type: G

  Description: Description for this RFC destination

  On the Technical Settings tab:

  Target: bn4l-i9u3ce9p.gtt-flp-lbnplatform.cfapps.eu10. hana.ondemand.com

  Port: 443

  Path Prefix: /api/idoc/em/v1/ TrackedProcessAndEvent

  (To send IDOC GTTMSG01 from S4 to BN4L GTT)

- On the Login & Security tab:

Logon Procedure

Logon with User: Basic Authentication with the technical user credentials is maintained. This technical user is also registered in SAP BN4L Global Track and Trace subaccount on the SAP BTP.

Logon with Ticket: Default value Do Not Send Logon Ticket.

Status of Secure Protocol: Active in SSL.

Figure 5-26. *GTT RFC destination*

It is advised to change the user email in the RFC to a separate technical user account which is not associated with any business user later.

Figure 5-27. *GTT RFC destination*

Status code "403" indicates the configuration is correct. No action is required.

Define Ports

System	SAP TM
Component/Module	BN4L GTT
SPRO Path	Display IMG page, click **Integration with Other SAP Components ➤ Interface to Global Track and Trace ➤ IDoc Settings.** Choose activity **Define Ports.**

In XML HTTP folder, a new port GTTAPPPORT is created with the following details:

RFC Destination: GTT_APP_RFC.

Content Type: application/x-sap.idoc.

HTTP Version: Version 1.0. SOAP Protocol is checked.

Figure 5-28. *Define port*

Define Partner Profiles

System	SAP TM System XX**
Component/Module	BN4L GTT
SPRO Path	In **Display IMG** page, unfold **Integration with Other SAP Components ➤ Interface to Global Track and Trace ➤ IDoc Settings.** Choose activity **Define Partner Profiles**

In the **Partner Type LS** folder, a new partner profile is created.

Figure 5-29. *Partner profile settings*

Under the **Outbound** box, a new outbound parameter is created. In the Message Type, GTTMSG and Receiver Port **GTTAPPPORT** are maintained.

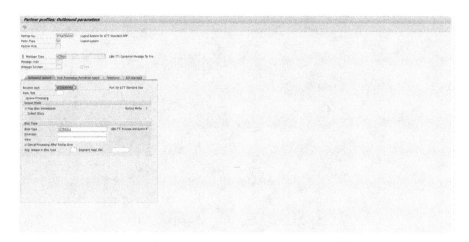

Figure 5-30. Partner profile settings

Freight Order Configuration

System	SAP TM
Component/Module	BN4L GTT
SPRO Path	In **Display IMG** page, **Transportation Management ➤ Freight Order Management ➤ Freight Order ➤ Define Freight Order Types**

In the **Integration Settings**, **Application Object Type** field with GTT_ SHP_HD application object is maintained.

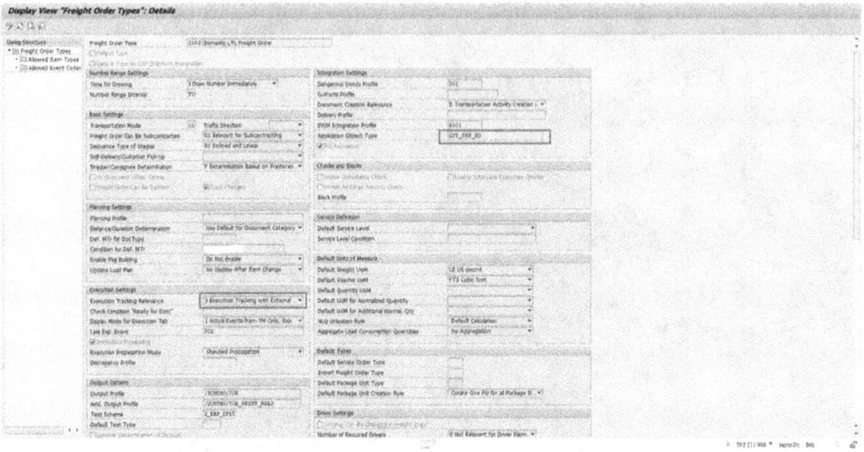

Figure 5-31. *Freight order type configuration*

Output Management Settings

To send the freight orders from TM to GTT, the below configuration was maintained:

System	SAP TM
Component/Module	BN4L GTT
SPRO Path	In **Display IMG** page, **Cross-Application Components** ➤ **Processes and Tools for Enterprise Applications** ➤ **Reusable Objects and Functions for BOPF Environment** ➤ **PPF Adapter for Output Management** ➤ **Maintain Output Management Adapter Settings**

In the **Dialog Structure** section, under **Direct Output Agents** (w/o PPF & w/o History).

168

Figure 5-32. *Output configuration*

Business Object	/SCMTMS/TOR
Node	ROOT
Output Agent	ZTM_OUTPUT_AGT_PRT
Action Profile	Z_TOR_PRINT_ROAD

Assign PPF Profiles	
Action Profile Des.	Custom FO Print Documents Road Freight
☑ Enable	
Output Type	Has Uncritical o/p: Process after Commit (background) ▼
Create DB Image	X Current Node ▼
☑ Preprocess Actions	
Agnt Class for Node	ZCL_TM_PRINTING

Figure 5-33. *Output configuration*

Freight Unit Configuration

System	SAP TM
Component/Module	BN4L GTT
SPRO Path	In **Display IMG** page, **Transportation Management ➤ Planning ➤ Freight Unit ➤ Define Freight Unit Types**

In the **Integration Settings**, **Application Object Type** field with GTT_ FU application object is maintained.

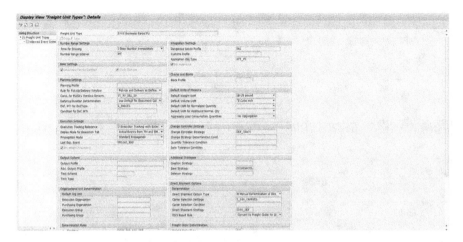

Figure 5-34. *Freight unit configuration*

Download ABAP Code

System	SAP TM System XX**
Component/Module	BN4L GTT

ABAPGit link: https://docs.abapgit.org/user-guide/getting-started/install.html

GTT objects download: https://github.com/SAP-samples/logistics-business-network-gtt-standardapps-samples.git

Figure 5-35. Download ABAP code

Technical Details

System	SAP TM System XX**
Component/Module	BN4L GTT

Packages:

GTT: Package for GTT LBN integration

GTT_STS: Standard tracking shipment

Custom Proxy Interface:

EVENT_TM_IN: To receive events from GTT to TM system

Classes:

GTTCL_ZEVENT_TM_IN: Service class

Z_TM_EVENT_IN: Service implementation class

Z_TM_EVENT_IN_SRV: Application class

ZCL_OM_UH_FACADE_EVR: Event manager update handler class

The following is the flow to update events:

1) ZGTTCL_ZEVENT_TM_IN:
   Read XI Message guide
   Create service implementation instance
   Execute service implementation
   Call FEH, if error occurred

2) Z_TM_EVENT_IN:
   Service-specific initializations
   Validation and mapping step
   Application processing

3) Z_TM_EVENT_IN_SRV:
   Check input message
   Get master data
   Fill data container for update handler
   Call update handler
   Create an entry in the communication history

4) ZCL_OM_UH_FACADE_EVR:
   Prepare TOR ROOT and TOR EXEC Data, and call the standard update handler /SCMTMS/CL_OM_ UH_FACADE ➤ EXECUTE_UPDATE_HANDLER.

Major code changes in

1) ZCL_GTT_STS_SEND_TOR_DATA ➤ GET_STOP_
    POSTAL_ADDR_INFO

    Postal Code Address cannot be retrieved directly
    from the Location Address Node since it is not
    available in TM 9.6 release.

    Hence, Address details are fetched through
    Geographical Information Node as below.

```
Method      GET_STOP_POSTAL_ADDR_INFO                                                   Active
40
41  □ *  SAP-GTT
42     *      lo_loc_srv_mgr->retrieve_by_association(
43     *          EXPORTING
44     *              iv_node_key      = /scmtms/if_location_c=>sc_node-root
45     *              it_key           = lt_location_key
46     *              iv_association   = /scmtms/if_location_c=>sc_association-root-address
47     *              iv_fill_data     = abap_true
48     *          IMPORTING
49     *              et_data          = lt_address_root
50     *              et_target_key    = lt_target_key ).
51
52          lo_loc_srv_mgr->retrieve_by_association(
53              EXPORTING
54                  iv_node_key      = /scmtms/if_location_c=>sc_node-root
55                  it_key           = lt_location_key
56                  iv_association   = /scmtms/if_location_c=>sc_association-root-geographical_information
57                  iv_fill_data     = abap_true
58              IMPORTING
59                  et_data          = lt_geo_root
60                  et_target_key    = lt_geo_key ).
61
```

Figure 5-36. *ABAP code placement*

2) ZCL_GTT_STS_TOOLS ➤ GET_POSTAL_ADDRESS

    Postal Code Address cannot be retrieved directly
    from the Location Address Node since it is not
    available in TM 9.6 release.

    Hence, Address details are fetched through
    Geographical Information Node as below.

Method	GET_POSTAL_ADDRESS	Active

```
22
23      IF lt_loc_log_key_link IS NOT INITIAL.
24  * SAP-GTT
25  *      lo_loc_srv_mgr->retrieve_by_association(
26  *        EXPORTING
27  *          iv_node_key      = /scmtms/if_location_c=>sc_node-root
28  *          it_key           = CORRESPONDING #( lt_loc_log_key_link MAPPING key = target_key )
29  *          iv_association = /scmtms/if_location_c=>sc_association-root-address
30  *        IMPORTING
31  *          et_key_link      = DATA(lt_address_key_link) ).
32
33        lo_loc_srv_mgr->retrieve_by_association(
34          EXPORTING
35            iv_node_key      = /scmtms/if_location_c=>sc_node-root
36            it_key           = CORRESPONDING #( lt_loc_log_key_link MAPPING key = target_key )
37            iv_association = /scmtms/if_location_c=>sc_association-root-geographical_information
38  *          iv_fill_data   = abap_true
39          IMPORTING
40            et_target_key = DATA(lt_geo_key) ).
```

Figure 5-37. *ABAP code placement*

   3)   ZCL_GTT_STS_TOOLS ➤ GET_SCAC_CODE

        Carrier SCAC code is retrieved from Table: BUT0ID
        instead of CDS view: /scmtms/cv_bpscac since this
        view is not available in TM 9.6 version.

Cross Tracked Process

When the freight unit is created or updated, to make sure its relationship
with its preceding delivery is updated, a new delivery header and item
IDOC needs to be generated and sent to the GTT system. This process
is internally referred to as "Cross TP process," and its process flow is as
follows.

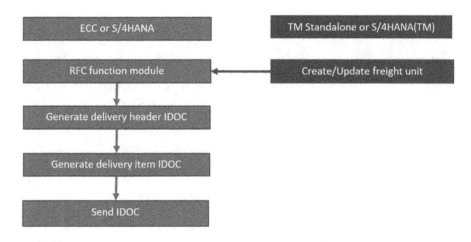

Figure 5-38. *Process flow*

TM system:

During the freight unit extraction to GTT, we introduced a method: GENERATE_DLV_IDOC.

Class Builder Class ZCL_GTT_STS_SEND_TOR_DATA Display

| Method | /SCMTMS/IF_SEND_TOR_DATA~CALL_EVENT_MGR |

```
115
116        generate_dlv_idoc(
117        EXPORTING
118          it_tor_root_sstring = it_tor_root_sstring
119          it_item_sstring = it_item_sstring
120        ).
```

Figure 5-39. *ABAP code placement*

In this method, if the freight unit item has ECC Delivery reference, then the same was passed to ECC system via RFC FM: ZGTT_CTP_TOR_TO_DLV.

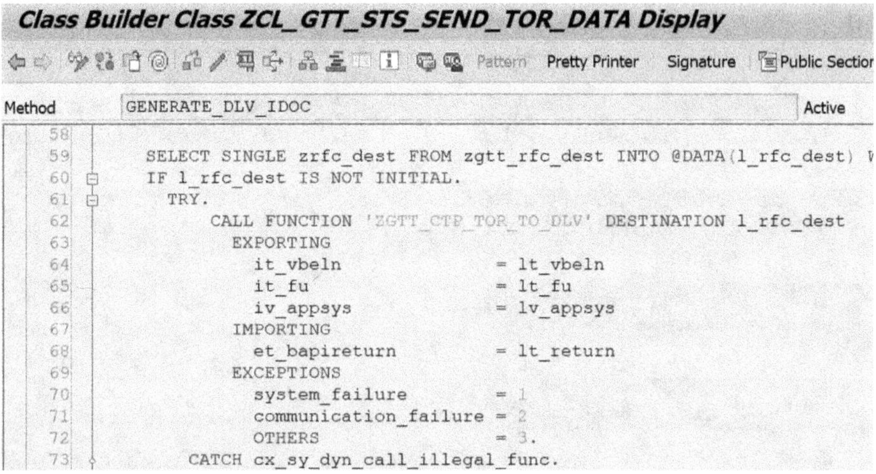

Class Builder Class ZCL_GTT_STS_SEND_TOR_DATA Display

Method	GENERATE_DLV_IDOC	Active

```
58
59      SELECT SINGLE zrfc_dest FROM zgtt_rfc_dest INTO @DATA(l_rfc_dest) W
60      IF l_rfc_dest IS NOT INITIAL.
61        TRY.
62          CALL FUNCTION 'ZGTT_CTP_TOR_TO_DLV' DESTINATION l_rfc_dest
63            EXPORTING
64              it_vbeln            = lt_vbeln
65              it_fu               = lt_fu
66              iv_appsys           = lv_appsys
67            IMPORTING
68              et_bapireturn       = lt_return
69            EXCEPTIONS
70              system_failure      = 1
71              communication_failure = 2
72              OTHERS              = 3.
73        CATCH cx_sy_dyn_call_illegal_func.
```

Figure 5-40. *ABAP code placement*

In ECC system: RFC: ZGTT_CTP_TOR_TO_DLV receives the delivery and its corresponding freight unit item data.

It builds the delivery header and item IDOC with its freight unit reference and sends to GTT.

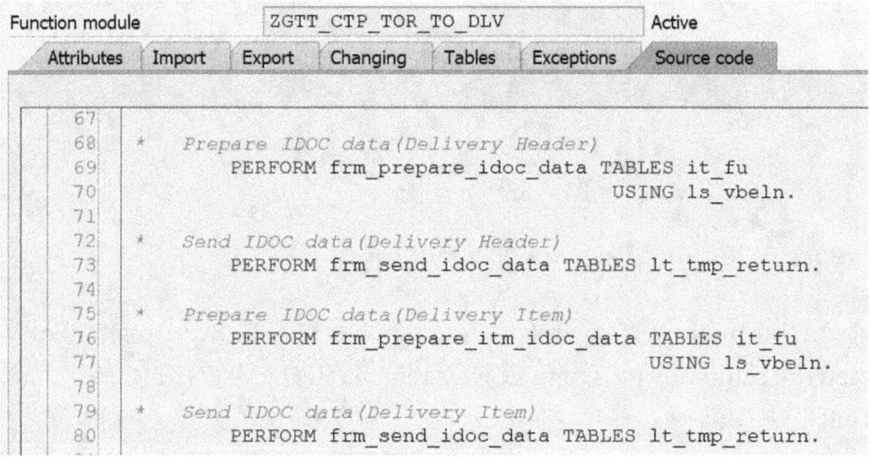

Function module	ZGTT_CTP_TOR_TO_DLV	Active

Attributes	Import	Export	Changing	Tables	Exceptions	Source code

```
67
68   *    Prepare IDOC data(Delivery Header)
69          PERFORM frm_prepare_idoc_data TABLES it_fu
70                                        USING ls_vbeln.
71
72   *    Send IDOC data(Delivery Header)
73          PERFORM frm_send_idoc_data TABLES lt_tmp_return.
74
75   *    Prepare IDOC data(Delivery Item)
76          PERFORM frm_prepare_itm_idoc_data TABLES it_fu
77                                            USING ls_vbeln.
78
79   *    Send IDOC data(Delivery Item)
80          PERFORM frm_send_idoc_data TABLES lt_tmp_return.
```

Figure 5-41. *ABAP code placement*

Also, in the Delivery Expected Events Method, instead of embedded TM call, we call side car TM system to get the TM relations.

FM: **ZGTT_SSOF_EE_DE_HD and ZGTT_SSOF_EE_DE_ITM**

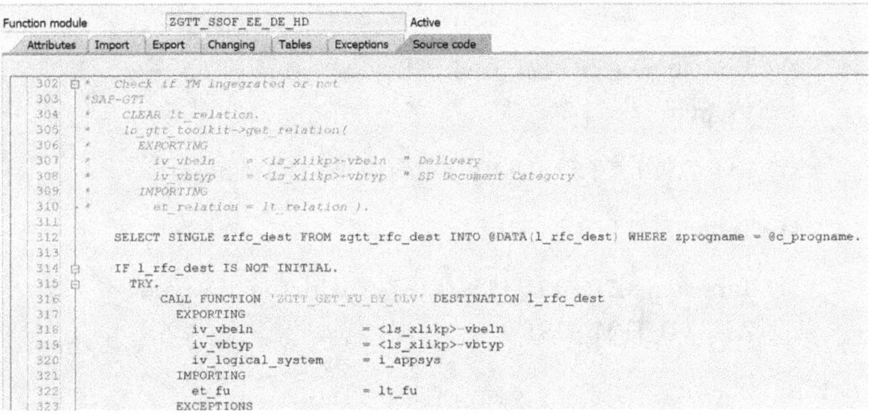

Figure 5-42. *ABAP code placement*

Also in FM: ZGTT_SSOF_OTE_DE_ITEM, we call the TM system to get the freight unit details to pass it on delivery item IDOC.

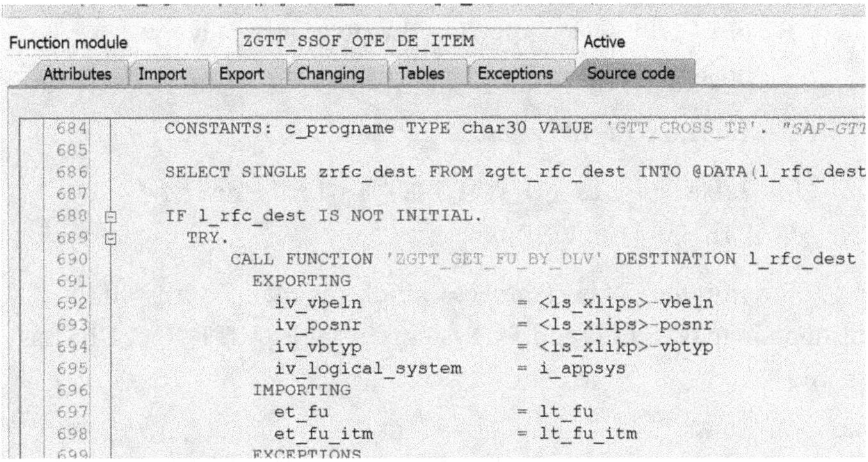

Figure 5-43. *ABAP code placement*

Development objects created:

TM system:

1) Table type **ZTS_FU_LIST_T** with the row type **ZTS_FU_LIST** in it

2) Table type **ZVBELN_T** with the line type **VBELN_VL** in it

3) FM: ZGTT_GET_FU_BY_DLV (to get TM relation)

4) Table: ZGTT_RFC_DEST

5) Table type **ZTS_FU_ITM_LIST_T** with the row type ZTS_FU_ITM_LIST in it

ECC system:

1) Table type **ZTS_FU_LIST_T** with the row type **ZTS_FU_LIST** in it

2) Table type **ZVBELN_T** with the line type **VBELN_VL** in it

3) FM: ZGTT_CTP_TOR_TO_DLV (to trigger delivery header and item IDOC)

4) Table: ZGTT_RFC_DEST

5) Table type **ZTS_FU_ITM_LIST_T** with the row type ZTS_FU_ITM_LIST in it

To support the Cross TP process, kindly maintain its cross RFC destination in both ECC and TM systems in Table: ZGTT_RFC_DEST as follows.

In ECC:

🗒 MANDT	ZPROGNAME	ZRFC_DEST
900	GTT_CROSS_TP	TP2CLNT900

Figure 5-44. *ABAP program assignment*

In TM:

🗒 MANDT	ZPROGNAME	ZRFC_DEST
900	GTT_CROSS_TP	EC2CLNT900

Figure 5-45. *ABAP program assignment*

Note   Cross TP Process is only developed for the following scenarios:

1) Sales Order ➤ Outbound Delivery ➤ Freight Unit ➤ Freight Order

2) Stock Transfer Order ➤ Outbound Delivery ➤ Freight Unit ➤ Freight Order

---

Summary

SAP BN4L is an advanced solution within the SAP ecosystem that provides businesses with comprehensive visibility into their supply chain activities, enabling real-time tracking, monitoring, and management of shipments and goods. Configuring **SAP BN4L** is essential to ensuring that businesses can optimize their logistics processes, handle exceptions efficiently, and gain actionable insights from their operations. The configuration process allows organizations to tailor BN4L to their specific needs, integrate it seamlessly with other SAP modules, Freight Collaboration, and track the movement and status of goods across the entire supply chain, from the supplier to the end customer.

This chapter outlines the key configuration details necessary to successfully set up **SAP BN4L** which involves several important steps that ensure the system works seamlessly and efficiently.

Configuration is a comprehensive process that plays a critical role in improving supply chain visibility, reducing delays, and enhancing overall logistics efficiency. The key steps in the configuration include system integration, defining tracking objects and milestones, setting up track and trace parameters, managing exceptions, configuring analytics and reporting, and ensuring security and compliance. Each of these components contributes to creating a powerful, integrated system that enables businesses to monitor shipments in real time, respond quickly to disruptions, and optimize their logistics operations.

By effectively configuring, businesses can gain deeper insights into their supply chain, enhance collaboration with partners, and improve customer satisfaction through better service delivery. As the global supply chain becomes increasingly complex, having the ability to trace and track goods in real time is essential for success. SAP BN4L helps organizations achieve this, providing them with the tools needed to navigate the challenges of modern logistics with confidence and precision.

This chapter has outlined the key configuration components of **SAP BN4L**, providing you with the necessary knowledge to set up and optimize your GTT system. By following these configuration steps, businesses can leverage the full potential of SAP BN4L to improve operational visibility, streamline decision-making, and create a more agile, responsive supply chain.

CHAPTER 6

Business Process

The transportation of goods is one of the most critical components of supply chain management, directly influencing customer satisfaction, cost efficiency, and operational agility. To streamline and optimize transportation processes, organizations rely on sophisticated technologies such as **SAP Transportation Management (SAP TM)** and **SAP BN4L**. These tools enable organizations to plan, execute, and monitor the movement of goods in real time, enhancing visibility, collaboration, and decision-making across the entire logistics network.

A crucial aspect of transportation management is the **Freight Order Confirmation by Carrier**. This process ensures that the transportation service provider or carrier acknowledges the receipt and acceptance of the freight order, providing confirmation of the transportation plan and initiating the execution of the transportation activities. Effective management of freight order confirmations allows businesses to monitor and control their transportation operations, ensuring that shipments are carried out according to plan and any exceptions are handled in a timely manner.

In this chapter, we will explore the process of **Freight Order Confirmation by Carrier** within the context of **SAP TM** and **SAP BN4L**. We will look at how these systems work together to facilitate seamless communication and collaboration between the shipper (the business) and the carrier, allowing for accurate planning, execution, and tracking of freight orders. We will also delve into the key configuration aspects, functionality, and benefits of this process within the SAP ecosystem.

© Prince Tyagi, Anevershika 2025
P. Tyagi and Anevershika, *Getting Started with BN4L and GTT Integrations for SAP*,
https://doi.org/10.1007/979-8-8688-1405-1_6

What Is Freight Order Confirmation by Carrier?

Freight Order Confirmation by Carrier is the process through which a carrier acknowledges a **freight order** created by a shipper in a transportation management system like **SAP TM**. A freight order represents a formal request from the shipper to the carrier to transport goods from one location to another, with specific details regarding the goods, transportation routes, and timelines.

The carrier's confirmation is essential for several reasons:

- **Assurance of Capacity**: The carrier confirms the availability of resources and capacity (e.g., trucks, containers, drivers) to carry out the transportation as per the order.

- **Start of Execution**: Confirmation marks the official commencement of the transportation process, with the carrier agreeing to the terms set forth in the freight order.

- **Visibility**: The confirmation provides both the shipper and the carrier with visibility into the transportation status, including any adjustments to the original transportation plan.

- **Communication**: The confirmation process facilitates clear and effective communication between the shipper and the carrier, ensuring alignment on the expectations for the shipment.

The Role of SAP TM in Freight Order Confirmation

SAP Transportation Management (SAP TM) is a comprehensive solution designed to manage the planning, execution, and optimization of transportation activities. Within **SAP TM**, freight orders play a central role in the transportation process. The shipper initiates the freight order in SAP TM, which contains all the details about the shipment, such as origin, destination, shipment type, required transportation modes, and deadlines.

The freight order confirmation by the carrier involves several steps in **SAP TM**:

1. **Carrier Selection**: The system selects the appropriate carrier for the freight order based on predefined criteria such as cost, capacity, service level, and route availability.

2. **Sending the Freight Order**: Once the carrier is selected, the system transmits the freight order to the carrier for confirmation. This is typically done electronically through a communication interface, which could be a **web service**, **EDI**, or **API**.

3. **Carrier Response**: The carrier receives the freight order and responds with a confirmation. The confirmation may include details such as the acceptance of the shipment, expected pick-up and delivery times, and any adjustments to the initial plan (e.g., changes in transportation modes or delays).

4. **Freight Order Update**: Based on the carrier's confirmation, SAP TM updates the freight order status, indicating whether the order has been confirmed, rejected, or requires further action. The system also tracks any exceptions or discrepancies between the planned and confirmed transportation details.

The carrier's confirmation in SAP TM ensures that both the shipper and the carrier are aligned in terms of expectations and responsibilities. It also provides the foundation for further transportation activities, such as scheduling, execution, and tracking.

SAP BN4L and Freight Order Confirmation

The **SAP BN4L** part of SAP's cloud-based logistics solutions enables seamless collaboration between various stakeholders in the logistics ecosystem, including suppliers, shippers, carriers, and logistics service providers. **SAP BN4L** enhances the traditional transportation management process by providing real-time visibility, improving collaboration, and facilitating data exchange between multiple parties.

In the context of **Freight Order Confirmation**, SAP BN4L serves as a hub for communication between the shipper and the carrier. The freight order that is created in **SAP TM** can be transmitted to the carrier through **SAP BN4L**, where it can be confirmed and updated. The platform leverages cloud-based technology and standard communication protocols, such as **APIs** and **web services**, to ensure that the freight order is delivered and confirmed in real time.

Here's how the process works with SAP BN4L:

1. **Freight Order Transmission**: After the shipper creates the freight order in **SAP TM**, it is sent to the **SAP BN4L** platform, where it can be accessed by the carrier.

2. **Carrier Confirmation**: The carrier logs into **SAP BN4L** or receives an automated notification, where they can confirm the details of the freight order, including the transportation capacity, schedules, and any required adjustments.

3. **Real-Time Updates**: Once the carrier confirms the order, **SAP BN4L** updates the status of the freight order in real time. This update is reflected in both **SAP TM** and **SAP BN4L**, providing both the shipper and carrier with accurate, up-to-date information.

4. **Exception Handling**: If the carrier cannot confirm the freight order due to capacity issues, route changes, or delays, the system can automatically flag the issue, allowing the shipper to take corrective action, such as reselecting a carrier or adjusting the transportation plan.

5. **Collaboration and Communication: SAP BN4L** also allows the shipper and carrier to communicate directly through the platform, sharing relevant documents (such as shipment details, bills of lading, and transport contracts) and updates. This improves collaboration, reduces errors, and accelerates decision-making.

SAP BN4L: Dispute and Invoicing

In the logistics and supply chain world, efficient invoicing and dispute management are crucial for maintaining strong relationships between businesses, service providers, and partners. SAP BN4L, also known as **SAP Logistics Business Network (LBN)**, is an advanced solution that facilitates seamless communication, collaboration, and data exchange across the entire logistics network. By streamlining processes such as invoicing and dispute resolution, SAP BN4L ensures that supply chain partners are paid promptly, discrepancies are quickly addressed, and the overall supply chain ecosystem runs smoothly.

In this article, we will explore how **SAP BN4L** helps organizations manage **disputes** and **invoicing** effectively, ensuring financial transparency, reducing operational friction, and optimizing the supply chain process.

The Importance of Dispute and Invoicing Management

In any supply chain, invoicing and payments represent significant operational processes that require accuracy, transparency, and timely resolution. Misunderstandings regarding shipment deliveries, payment terms, pricing discrepancies, and other logistical challenges can often lead to disputes. These disputes, if not resolved promptly, can delay payments, negatively affect business relationships, and result in unnecessary administrative overhead.

Efficient invoicing ensures that businesses pay their partners correctly, while effective dispute resolution minimizes financial friction and ensures that operational disruptions do not escalate into long-term conflicts. The ability to automate and manage both aspects through **SAP BN4L** is essential for improving cash flow, maintaining positive business relationships, and avoiding costly delays in the supply chain.

SAP BN4L and Its Role in Dispute and Invoicing Management

SAP BN4L acts as a collaborative platform that brings together supply chain stakeholders, including suppliers, logistics providers, and shippers, into a unified network. By leveraging this platform, companies can handle invoicing and dispute management more efficiently, reduce manual processes, and enhance visibility into financial transactions and operations. Here's how SAP BN4L aids in managing these critical aspects.

Invoicing Process in SAP BN4L

The invoicing process within **SAP BN4L** revolves around the seamless exchange of transactional data between all parties involved. The system helps automate the creation, verification, and processing of invoices, eliminating the need for manual intervention and reducing the likelihood of errors.

Key aspects of the invoicing process in SAP BN4L include

- **Automated Invoice Generation**: When goods are delivered or transportation services are completed, SAP BN4L enables automatic creation of invoices based on the contractual agreement between the parties. The system can use data from **SAP TM**, **SAP S/4HANA**, and other integrated systems to generate invoices directly from transaction records.

- **Invoice Validation**: Once an invoice is generated, SAP BN4L helps validate it by comparing the information on the invoice (e.g., amounts, services rendered, dates) with the relevant shipment details, contracts, and agreements. This ensures accuracy and consistency across all transactional data.

- **Invoice Exchange**: The platform facilitates real-time exchange of invoices between shippers and carriers or third-party logistics (3PL) providers. The use of electronic invoicing methods, such as **EDI** (Electronic Data Interchange) or **APIs**, ensures that invoices are transmitted promptly and securely.

- **Invoice Discrepancy Handling**: If discrepancies are found in the invoice (e.g., incorrect amounts, unapproved charges), SAP BN4L allows for the automatic identification and resolution of issues. The system flags discrepancies for further investigation, enabling faster processing of corrected invoices.

- **Payment Tracking**: SAP BN4L integrates with financial systems to track payment status, providing visibility into pending payments and outstanding invoices. This helps businesses manage their cash flow and ensures timely payments to vendors and service providers.

Dispute Management in SAP BN4L

Disputes are inevitable in complex supply chains, but **SAP BN4L** provides tools for identifying, managing, and resolving disputes efficiently. The dispute management features of SAP BN4L ensure that any invoicing issues, delivery discrepancies, or other disputes are addressed quickly, minimizing the impact on business relationships and operations.

Key aspects of the dispute management process in SAP BN4L include

- **Dispute Identification and Logging**: If there is an issue with an invoice or shipment, such as a pricing error, late delivery, or incorrect service charges, stakeholders can log the dispute directly in the **SAP BN4L** platform. The system tracks these disputes by capturing the reason, details, and evidence, such as shipment logs or service records.

- **Automated Alerts and Notifications**: Once a dispute is logged, **SAP BN4L** sends automated alerts and notifications to the relevant parties, such as logistics managers or financial departments, informing them of the dispute and the necessary steps for resolution. These alerts ensure that issues are addressed quickly and don't fall through the cracks.

- **Collaboration and Communication**: The platform enables real-time communication between all stakeholders involved in the dispute resolution process. Whether it's a carrier disputing charges, a shipper questioning delivery times, or a supplier disputing payment terms, SAP BN4L provides a collaborative environment where all relevant documents (e.g., contracts, invoices, shipment records) can be shared and discussed.

- **Root Cause Analysis**: By using data from SAP systems such as **SAP TM** and **SAP S/4HANA**, businesses can conduct a detailed analysis to identify the root cause of the dispute. For instance, if a shipment is delayed, SAP BN4L can provide data on the transport planning, execution, and actual delivery times, helping the parties identify whether the issue was related to the carrier, warehouse, or external factors.

- **Dispute Resolution Workflow**: SAP BN4L supports the creation of structured workflows for dispute resolution. These workflows define the steps needed to resolve an issue, such as negotiations, the exchange of supporting documentation, or approvals for adjusted charges. Workflows can be customized to fit the specific needs of each organization and dispute type, ensuring a standardized and efficient approach to dispute resolution.

- **Audit Trail and Documentation**: Throughout the dispute resolution process, SAP BN4L maintains a complete audit trail of all activities and communications. This documentation can be used for future reference, helping businesses track patterns in disputes, identify recurring issues, and develop strategies for preventing similar problems in the future.

- **Chapter: BN4L (LBN)—Events from Carrier Tenant**

  In the complex world of logistics, the ability to track, monitor, and manage the movement of goods across the supply chain is vital. Events such as shipments, delays, and exceptions play a critical role in ensuring the efficient flow of operations. **SAP BN4L (SAP BN4L)**, also known as **SAP Logistics Business Network (LBN)**, is a powerful cloud-based platform designed to streamline collaboration among various stakeholders in the logistics ecosystem, including suppliers, logistics service providers, carriers, and shippers.

One of the key features of **SAP BN4L** is its ability to handle **events** originating from the **Carrier Tenant**. The **Carrier Tenant** refers to the digital presence of a logistics carrier within the SAP BN4L network, where they can access and share data related to transportation, delivery schedules, milestones, exceptions, and more. This chapter will explore the concept of **events from the Carrier Tenant**, detailing their types, how they are captured and processed within **SAP BN4L**, and the benefits they provide to all supply chain stakeholders.

Introduction to Events from Carrier Tenant in SAP BN4L

In the context of **SAP BN4L**, an **event** represents a specific occurrence or action related to a shipment or logistics activity that provides valuable insight into the transportation process. Events can include activities like **shipment departures**, **arrival notifications**, **delays**, **customs clearance**, **loading/unloading status**, or **exception reports**. These events are generated by the carrier when significant milestones are achieved or when issues arise during the transportation process.

The **Carrier Tenant** in SAP BN4L is the digital representation of the carrier or logistics service provider in the network. It allows carriers to interact with the broader supply chain network, receive transportation orders, provide real-time updates on shipments, and report events. When an event occurs within the carrier's operations (e.g., a shipment reaches a new milestone), the carrier can report this event back to **SAP BN4L**, which processes and broadcasts it to all relevant stakeholders.

By using **events from the Carrier Tenant**, organizations can gain enhanced visibility into the status of shipments, improve communication with logistics partners, and proactively manage exceptions. This results in improved efficiency, better decision-making, and a more agile supply chain.

- **Types of Events from the Carrier Tenant**

  Events from the Carrier Tenant in **SAP BN4L** are categorized into different types, depending on the stage of transportation and the specific actions taken by the carrier. These events reflect the progress of a shipment, provide insights into exceptions, and ensure that all involved parties are informed in real time. Below are the main types of events that originate from the **Carrier Tenant**:

  - **Departure Events**

    A **departure event** is triggered when a shipment begins its journey, either leaving a warehouse, manufacturing facility, or consolidation point. This event informs all relevant stakeholders that the shipment is en route. The departure event typically includes critical information such as

    - **Departure location**

    - **Date and time of departure**

    - **Carrier identification**

    - **Transport mode**

    The **departure event** provides the first milestone in the transportation journey and is essential for tracking the goods' movement. This event helps logistics planners monitor the start of transportation activities and make necessary adjustments if there are issues with the shipment's departure.

- **Arrival Events**

  An **arrival event** is triggered when the shipment arrives at its destination, whether it be a customer site, warehouse, or port. It provides stakeholders with the real-time status of a shipment's arrival, including

  - **Arrival location**

  - **Date and time of arrival**

  - **Shipment identification**

  - **Transport mode**

  The **arrival event** is crucial for assessing the performance of the shipment and evaluating whether it was delivered on time. It also serves as a key point in inventory management, as it indicates that the goods are ready for unloading, inspection, or further processing.

- **Milestone Events**

  Milestone events represent significant points or milestones during the transportation process, such as reaching a certain location, completing a key step in the journey (e.g., customs clearance), or finishing loading or unloading processes. These events can be generated at various stages of the transportation journey and are used to update stakeholders on the progress of a shipment.

Common examples of **milestone events** include

- **Customs clearance completed**

- **Delivery completed at a distribution center**

- **Loading completed at the origin facility**

- **Unloading completed at the destination facility**

Milestone events are useful for managing customer expectations, tracking performance, and verifying whether transportation timelines are being met.

- **Exception Events**

  Exception events occur when deviations from the planned transportation process are identified. These events are particularly important for proactive decision-making, as they alert stakeholders to potential issues that could affect the delivery timeline, cost, or quality of service.

  Examples of **exception events** include

  - **Shipment Delay**: A delay due to unforeseen circumstances such as weather, traffic, or operational issues

  - **Damaged Goods**: Notification that the goods have been damaged during transit or handling

  - **Missing Documents**: A report indicating missing or incomplete customs documents that may delay shipment processing

The **exception event** plays a key role in managing disruptions and helping supply chain stakeholders take corrective actions. The earlier an exception is identified, the more effectively it can be addressed.

- **Transit and In-Transit Events**

  Transit events provide real-time updates on the movement of goods while in transit. These events capture data on the current status of a shipment as it travels between locations. For example:

  - **In-Transit Checkpoint Updates**: The shipment passes through a customs checkpoint or another key location.

  - **Current Location and Estimated Time of Arrival (ETA)**: A real-time update on the shipment's location and expected arrival time.

  These events are essential for keeping track of the shipment's progress and ensuring accurate, up-to-date tracking information. They allow businesses to provide customers with accurate ETAs and manage the logistics process with higher precision.

- **Capturing and Reporting Events from the Carrier Tenant**

  Events from the **Carrier Tenant** are captured and reported in **SAP BN4L** using various methods and integration technologies. The **Carrier Tenant** communicates with **SAP BN4L** through standard data exchange protocols, such as **APIs**, **EDI**, or **web services**, enabling the real-time transmission of event data.

Here's how events are typically captured and reported:

1. **Data Capture:** As events occur within the carrier's operations (e.g., departure, arrival, delay), the carrier records these actions within their own systems or devices (e.g., GPS trackers, mobile apps).

2. **Event Transmission:** Once an event is captured, it is transmitted from the Carrier Tenant to **SAP BN4L**. The transmission may happen in real time or at scheduled intervals, depending on the configuration.

3. **Event Processing: SAP BN4L** processes the event data and integrates it into the broader logistics network. The platform automatically updates relevant stakeholders about the event, triggering workflows or alerts as needed.

4. **Stakeholder Notification:** Once the event is processed, relevant stakeholders, such as shippers, warehouse managers, and supply chain analysts, are notified. They can access event details through their SAP system or via the **SAP BN4L** portal.

- **Benefits of Events from Carrier Tenant in SAP BN4L**

   The reporting and management of events originating from the **Carrier Tenant** provide numerous benefits for businesses and their supply chain operations, including

195

- **Enhanced Visibility**

  Events provide end-to-end visibility into the transportation process, enabling businesses to monitor the status of shipments at every stage of the journey. This visibility is critical for decision-makers to proactively manage their supply chain operations, mitigate risks, and meet customer expectations.

- **Real-Time Information**

  The real-time nature of event reporting ensures that all stakeholders have access to the most up-to-date information regarding shipment progress. This allows businesses to take immediate action in case of delays, exceptions, or other issues that could affect delivery times.

- **Improved Customer Satisfaction**

  By leveraging events from the **Carrier Tenant**, businesses can provide their customers with accurate and timely updates on their orders, improving communication and transparency. The ability to notify customers of potential delays or disruptions enables companies to manage expectations and offer proactive solutions.

- **Better Exception Management**

  Exception events allow businesses to quickly identify issues and take corrective action. By addressing disruptions promptly, companies can minimize the impact on delivery schedules and prevent minor issues from escalating into larger problems.

- **Data-Driven Decision-Making**

  Events from the Carrier Tenant feed valuable data
  into the organization's decision-making process.
  By analyzing the data from events, businesses
  can optimize their logistics operations, improve
  planning, and refine their carrier selection criteria
  based on performance metrics.

BN4L (LBN): Freight Order Confirmation by Carrier

Freight Order Creation: The shipper creates a freight order in the SAP
Transportation Management (TM) system. This order contains all the
necessary details about the shipment, such as the origin, destination, and
cargo specifications.

The section is created at the sub-process level. This document will be
covering process flow with the navigation steps helping in running the
cycle in SAP system.

This document talks of performing direct tendering or subcontracting
of freight orders with SAP Logistics Business Network.

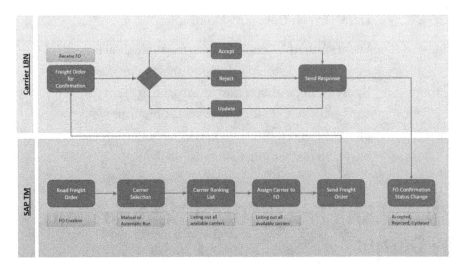

Figure 6-1. *FO confirmation process flow*

Access the activity using one of the following navigation options:

SAP Menu	*Carrier Tenant* ➤ *Freight Order Management* ➤ *Freight Orders for Confirmation*

Workflow Steps

Sending Freight Order to Carrier: The freight order is sent to the carrier via the SAP LBN platform. This can be done through direct tendering or a request for quotation (RFQ) process, depending on the shipper's configuration.

Step 1: Document Verification

There should not be any carrier assigned to freight order.

Screenshot from SAP TM

Figure 6-2. *Freight order Fiori screen*

Step 2: Carrier Selection

Carriers can be selected either manually or automatically:

- **Manual Selection**: The user assigns a carrier to the freight order based on predefined criteria, such as cost, priority, or capacity.

- **Automatic Selection**: The system uses optimization algorithms to evaluate carriers based on factors like cost, priority, transportation allocation, and business share. It then generates a ranked list of carriers and selects the most suitable one.

Trigger Carrier Selection manually by clicking the "Carrier Selection" button to display carriers in the carrier ranking list. The carrier receives the freight order and reviews the details, including the transport requirements, timelines, and any additional instructions.

Screenshot from SAP TM

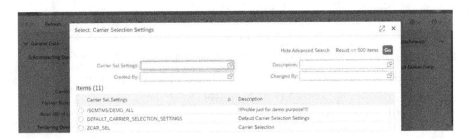

Figure 6-3. *Freight order Fiori screen*

2.1. **Carrier Selection Settings:** The Carrier Selection
Settings in SAP Transportation Management (SAP
TM) is a critical configuration tool that determines
how carriers are selected for freight orders. It allows
businesses to define rules and strategies for assigning
the most suitable carrier based on various criteria.
Here's an overview of its key aspects:

Choose the relevant "carrier selection" settings
from the drop-down list.

Screenshot from SAP TM

Figure 6-4. *Freight order Fiori screen*

2.2. Carrier Ranking List:

The **carrier ranking list** in SAP Transportation Management (SAP TM) is a feature that helps prioritize carriers based on predefined criteria, ensuring the most suitable carrier is selected for a freight order. See if there are available carriers in the carrier ranking list.

Screenshot from SAP TM

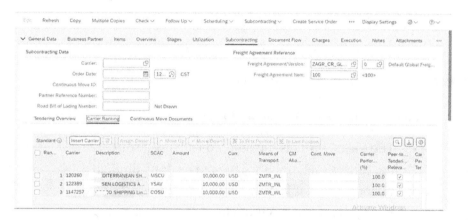

Figure 6-5.   *Freight order Fiori screen*

Step 3: Carrier Assignment

There are two options for the next step.

3.1. Start the tendering process to check carrier availability (this step is covered in tendering manual user guide).

3.2. Assign the carrier directly by highlighting the relevant carrier and clicking the "Assign Carrier" button.

Screenshot from SAP TM

Figure 6-6. *Freight order Fiori screen*

Step 4: Sending Freight Order to Carrier

- The freight order is transmitted with this feature to the carrier via SAP LBN. This can be done through various communication methods, such as APIs or EDI (Electronic Data Interchange), depending on the carrier's integration setup.

- The carrier receives the freight order in their LBN portal or integrated system.

4.1. Single Order "Send to Carrier":

Send the freight order to the carrier by clicking "Send to Carrier" in Subcontracting.

Screenshot from SAP TM

Figure 6-7. *Freight order Fiori screen*

4.2. **Mass "Send to Carrier":**

In SAP Transportation Management (SAP TM), the **Freight Order Worklist** is a tool that provides an overview of all freight orders and their statuses, allowing users to manage and process them efficiently. The **"Send to Carrier"** option is a key feature within this worklist, enabling the communication of freight orders to carriers. Here's how it works:

1. **Accessing the Freight Order Worklist:**

   - The Freight Order Worklist can be accessed through the SAP TM interface, typically under the Transportation Cockpit or a similar module.

   - It displays a list of freight orders, including details such as order numbers, statuses, assigned carriers, and shipment details.

2. **Selecting a Freight Order:**

- Users can select one or multiple freight orders from the worklist that need to be sent to carriers.

- The selection can be based on criteria such as shipment priority, deadlines, or carrier availability.

3. **Using the "Send to Carrier" Option:**

- Once the freight order is selected, the "Send to Carrier" option is used to initiate the communication process.

- This action triggers the system to send the freight order details to the assigned carrier via the configured communication method (e.g., EDI, XML, or API).

4. **Carrier Notification:**

- The carrier receives the freight order in their system or through the SAP Logistics Business Network (LBN) portal.

- They can review the order details and confirm acceptance or provide feedback if necessary.

5. **Monitoring and Updates:**

- The Freight Order Worklist is updated with the carrier's response, such as confirmation or rejection.

- Users can monitor the status of the freight order and take further actions if required.

This feature streamlines the process of assigning and communicating freight orders, ensuring efficient collaboration between shippers and carriers.

You can send multiple freight orders to relevant LBN carriers for confirmation using the Freight Order worklist as shown below.

Screenshot from SAP TM

Figure 6-8. *Freight order worklist Fiori screen*

Select the relevant freight orders which have the LBN Carrier assigned, click "Subcontracting" drop-down, and select "Send to Carrier."

Screenshot from SAP TM

Figure 6-9. *Freight order worklist Fiori screen*

Users can get to know which freight orders were sent to the carrier by verifying the "Subcontracting Status" of the freight order as "**SENT.**" Please refer to the worklist screenshot below.

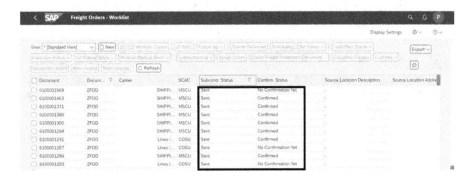

Figure 6-10. *Freight order worklist Fiori screen*

Step 5: Notifications for Freight Order Confirmation

5.1. **SAP LBN Carrier Tenant**:

LBN Carrier Tenant receives the notification in "Freight Orders for Confirmation" tile.

Figure 6-11. *Freight order confirmation application screen*

5.2. **User Email Notification**:

If users having access to Carrier Tenant are subscribed (using their email address) to the event of "Create Freight Order for Confirmation," "Update Freight Order for Confirmation," and "Cancel Freight Order for Confirmation" in the "DEFINE USER SETTINGS" app, then they would receive standard email notifications from LBN tenant whenever a freight order is sent for confirmation, updated after it is sent for confirmation, or cancelled after being sent for confirmation.

Figure 6-12. *Email notification*

User received a mail from saplbn@mailsap.com"New Order notification-Freight Order XXXXXX received from Shipper XYZ-USA for your response.

Step 6: Carrier Action

The **Freight Order Confirmation Application** on SAP Logistics Business Network (LBN) is a key tool that facilitates seamless collaboration between shippers and carriers. Here's an overview of its functionality and process:

1. **Freight Order Transmission**

   - Freight orders created in SAP Transportation Management (TM) are sent to carriers via SAP LBN.

   - The application ensures that carriers receive all relevant details, such as shipment origin, destination, cargo specifications, and timelines.

2. **Carrier Review and Confirmation**

   - Carriers access the freight orders through the LBN portal or their integrated systems.

   - They can review the order details and confirm acceptance. If necessary, carriers can update specific information, such as vehicle and driver details.

There are two options for the next step (please note that you cannot change operational data, e.g., date/time in tour, product, etc.).

   6.1. Accept FO by Carrier

      6.1.1. Check if all information (e.g., tour, cargo, booking details in Notes, etc.) is correct, and if needed, add information in the "Notes" tab, attach document in the "Attachments" tab, or add information in the "Drivers and License Plate" tab.

      6.1.2. If everything is correct, click "Confirm."

Screenshot from SAP LBN Carrier Tenant

Figure 6-13. *Freight order confirmation application screen*

6.1.3. Check if you can display FO under the
"Responded To (Open)" tab.

Screenshot from SAP LBN Carrier Tenant

Figure 6-14. *Freight order confirmation application screen*

6.1.4. Check if you receive FO confirmation in SAP TM, and see if confirmation status changes from "No Confirmation Yet" to "Confirmed."

Screenshot from SAP TM

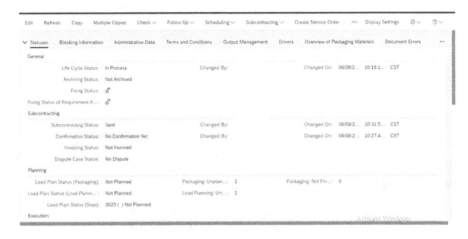

Figure 6-15. *Freight order Status tab screen*

Figure 6-16. *Freight order Status tab screen*

6.1.5. If the carrier wants to send any update (or reject) after confirmation, the carrier needs to change information in the corresponding FO under the "Responded To (Open)" tab, and click the "Send Update" button.

Screenshot from SAP LBN Carrier Tenant

Figure 6-17. *Freight order confirmation LBN screen*

Figure 6-18. *Freight order confirmation LBN screen*

6.2. Reject FO by Carrier

(Please note that another FO was created to show reject functionality.)

6.2.1. Please repeat steps 6.1.1, 6.1.2, and 6.1.3, but "reject" FO in Carrier Tenant.

Screenshot from SAP LBN Carrier Tenant

Figure 6-19. *Freight order confirmation LBN screen*

Please repeat steps and verify "Rejected" status in FO on SAP TM side.

Screenshot from SAP TM

Figure 6-20. *Freight order status screen*

BN4L (LBN): Dispute and Invoicing

The **Dispute and Invoicing Application** in SAP Logistics Business Network (LBN) is designed to streamline the invoicing process and manage disputes effectively between shippers and carriers. Here's an overview of its functionality:

1. **Invoicing Process**

    -   Carriers can create and submit invoices for freight orders directly through the SAP LBN platform.

    -   The system ensures that the charges in the invoice match the freight order details. If discrepancies are found, the system flags them for review.

2. **Dispute Management**

- When there are mismatches between the invoice charges and the agreed terms, the system generates a dispute document.

- Disputes can be reviewed and resolved within the LBN platform. The shipper can either accept the changes or reject them, providing reasons for the decision.

3. **Integration with SAP TM**

- The invoicing and dispute processes are integrated with SAP Transportation Management (TM), ensuring seamless data exchange and synchronization.

- Updates made in the LBN platform are reflected in the SAP TM system, maintaining consistency across platforms.

4. **Applications for Management**

- The **Invoice Freight Documents App** allows carriers to view freight orders ready for invoicing and create invoices.

- The **Manage Invoices App** enables carriers to track the status of submitted invoices.

- The **Manage Disputes App** provides tools for reviewing and resolving disputes efficiently.

5. **Real-Time Updates**

- The system provides real-time notifications and updates to stakeholders, ensuring transparency and proactive communication.

This is the drayage scenario where we have the source location as a warehouse and the destination location as a seaport. Steps A and B are mandatory for creating an invoice or a dispute.

A. Send freight order for confirmation to the carrier from SAP TM. Once the carrier confirms the FO in Carrier Tenant, the confirmation status will be set to **"Confirmed"** on FO.

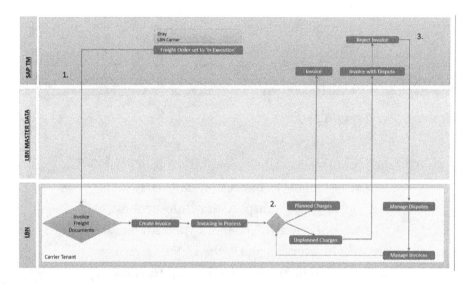

Figure 6-21. *Dispute process*

Access the activity using one of the following navigation options:

SAP Menu	*Invoicing : LBN Carrier Tenant ➤ Freight Settlement ➤ Invoice Freight Documents*
	Dispute : LBN Carrier Tenant ➤ Freight Settlement ➤ Manage Disputes

Screenshot from SAP TM

Figure 6-22.   *Freight order*

B.   Once confirmed, set the execution status of FO in
SAP TM system to **"In Execution"** and save. On
save, webservices:TransportationOrderRequest_Out
and TransportationOrderGenericTrackedProcess
Request_Out are triggered to the LBN system. The
FO will appear in the **"Invoice Freight Documents"**
Fiori tile in Carrier Tenant.

1.   **Steps to Invoice Freight Document**

You can view all the freight documents that are
ready for invoicing using the **Invoice Freight
Documents** app.

The **Invoice Freight Documents** app consists of
a main view and a detail view.

When you launch the app, the system displays
the main view with the following areas:

- Filter Bar

  Using the filter bar in the header, you can
  filter the freight documents to restrict the
  number of freight documents displayed. You
  can filter based on one or more of the freight
  document details such as freight document,
  departure date, departure location, arrival
  date, arrival location, customer account,
  reference document ID, reference document
  type, changed on, created on, gross amount,
  and gross amount currency details.

- Worklists

  You can use the following worklists: **To be
  Invoiced**, **Invoicing in Process**, **Completely
  Invoiced**, and **All**.

  To create an invoice, you must select a freight
  document (e.g., using FO 6100001204) from the
  worklist page and choose **Create Invoice**.

  Alternatively, you can also choose **Create
  Invoice** on the header area of the detail view of
  a freight document.

  You can also select multiple freight documents
  from the worklist page and choose **Create
  Invoice**. The system creates individual invoices,
  one each for all the selected freight documents.

  Note that if you already have an invoice in draft
  version for a freight document, you cannot
  create a new invoice.

Screenshot from SAP LBN Carrier Tenant

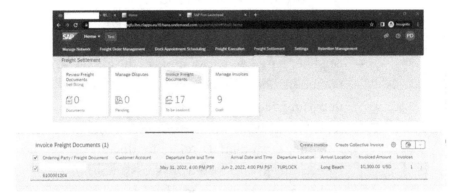

Figure 6-23. *Invoice application*

The below screen would appear. Provide a
different invoice ID in the highlighted field.

Screenshot from SAP LBN Carrier Tenant

Figure 6-24. *Invoice application*

The carrier can attach files under the
Attachments section as shown below.

Screenshot from SAP LBN Carrier Tenant

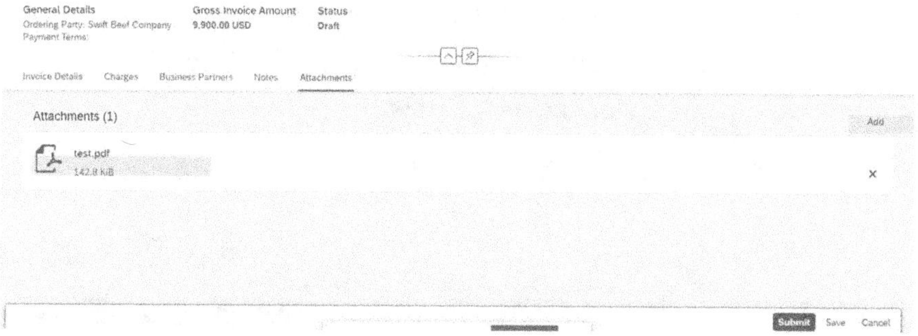

Figure 6-25. Invoice application

The carrier can add notes in the **Notes section**
as well, before submitting the invoice.

Screenshot from SAP LBN Carrier Tenant

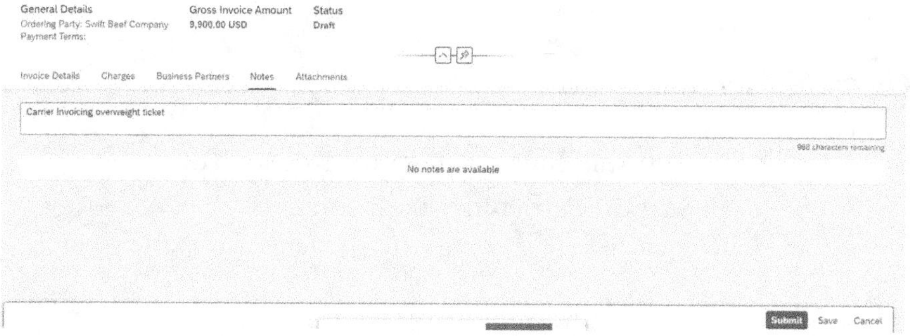

Figure 6-26. Invoice application

On this screen, click "Submit" to create the invoice.

As soon as you click the "Submit" button, the system would trigger web service **InvoiceRequest_In** in the background to create an invoice in SAP TM system. The invoice will appear in the document flow of FO in the SAP TM system as seen below.

Screenshot from SAP TM

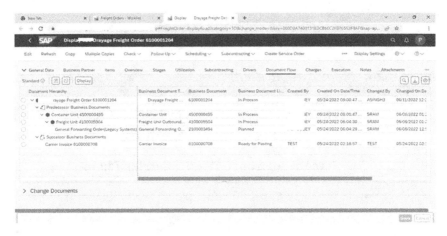

***Figure 6-27.** Freight order*

Note was updated under the Notes tab of the SAP TM Carrier Invoice document.

Screenshot from SAP TM

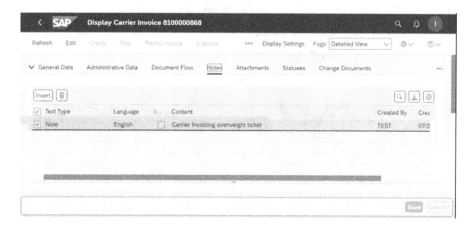

Figure 6-28. *Freight order*

Attachments are updated under the "Attachments" tab of the SAP TM Carrier Invoice document.

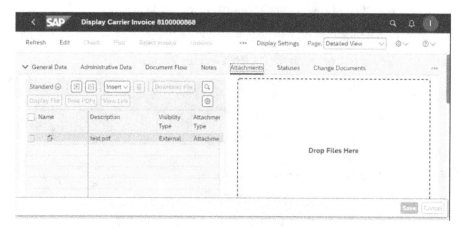

Figure 6-29. *Freight order*

2. **Steps for Dispute Creation**

If there is a freight order to be Invoiced, and you wish to create a dispute, navigate to the "Invoice Freight Document" Fiori tile.

Screenshot from SAP LBN Carrier Tenant

Figure 6-30. *LBN invoice application*

From the above Fiori tile, select the FO for which you wish to create a dispute. I am using FO 6100001211; select the freight order, and click the "Create Invoice" button.

Screenshot from SAP LBN Carrier Tenant

Figure 6-31. *LBN invoice application*

The below screen would appear. Provide a different invoice ID in the highlighted field.

Screenshot from SAP LBN Carrier Tenant

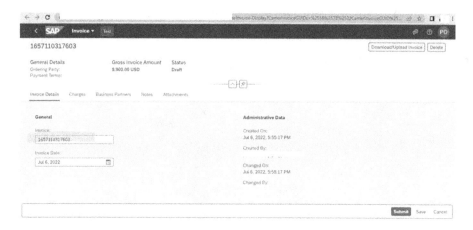

Figure 6-32. LBN invoice application

In this screen, navigate to the Charges tab. Make changes in the charges. You can modify already existing values and also add another charge type if required. Make sure to populate the same values in both Rate Amount and Final Amount columns, if editable.

Changes that can be made in charges:

Modify Existing Charges

To modify the charges of the existing charge type, propose the new amount under the Rate Amount column (enter the same amount again in Final Amount).

Screenshot from SAP LBN Carrier Tenant

Figure 6-33. LBN invoice application

Add Another Charge Type to the List

You can also add charge types to the list. In order
to do so, select the "Add" drop-down present on
the right corner of the table. Select charge from the
drop-down.

Screenshot from SAP LBN Carrier Tenant

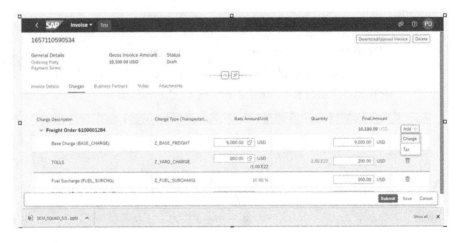

Figure 6-34. LBN invoice application

A blank line would be added to the screen.

Screenshot from SAP LBN Carrier Tenant

Figure 6-35. *LBN invoice application*

Click Help to get the list of possible unplanned charges.

Screenshot from SAP LBN Carrier Tenant

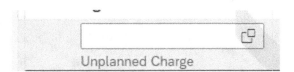

Figure 6-36. *LBN invoice application*

Choose from the list to proceed.

Screenshot from SAP LBN Carrier Tenant

Figure 6-37. *LBN invoice application*

Give the desired charge against the unplanned charge type just added. This is how user can add additional unplanned charges.

Screenshot from SAP LBN Carrier Tenant

Figure 6-38. *LBN invoice application*

Remove a Charge

To remove a charge, use the red bin icon present at the rightmost column of the charges table.

Screenshot from SAP LBN Carrier Tenant

Figure 6-39. *LBN invoice application*

After making appropriate changes, proceed to completion by pressing the "Submit" button. This will submit the invoice.

Screenshot from SAP LBN Carrier Tenant

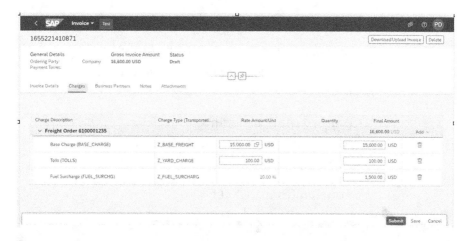

Figure 6-40. *LBN invoice application*

As soon as you submit the dispute, the system would trigger web service **InvoiceRequest_In** to create a dispute in SAP TM. The dispute and invoice will appear in the document flow of FO in the SAP TM system as seen below.

Screenshot from SAP TM

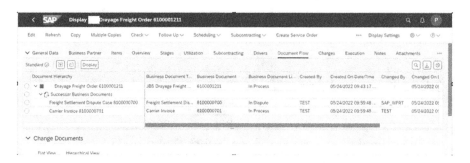

Figure 6-41. *Freight order*

3. **Steps for Invoice Rejection**

If the ordering party wishes to reject the disputed
amount from the carrier, they need to follow the
below steps.

1. To proceed with Carrier Invoice rejection,
cancel the dispute, and cancel the invoice at
SAP TM end.

Screenshot from SAP TM

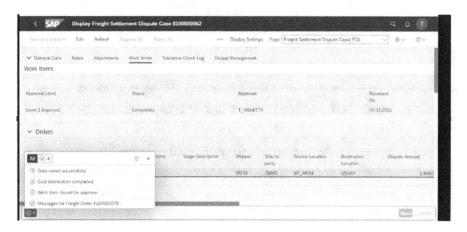

Figure 6-42. *Freight settlement*

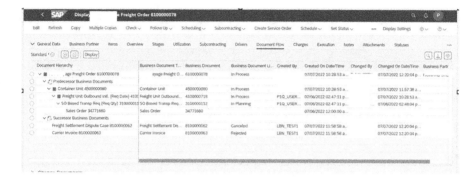

Figure 6-43. *Freight order*

TM sends communication to LBN and creates
a dispute under Manage Disputes Fiori App for
Carrier Tenant.

2. The carrier can find the new dispute under
    the to be approved status tab of the "Manage
    Disputes" Fiori App.

Screenshot from SAP LBN Carrier Tenant

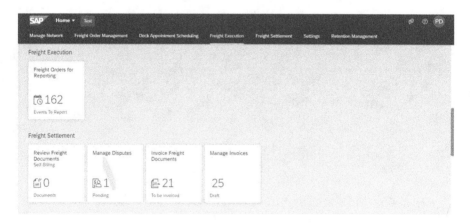

Figure 6-44. *LBN screen*

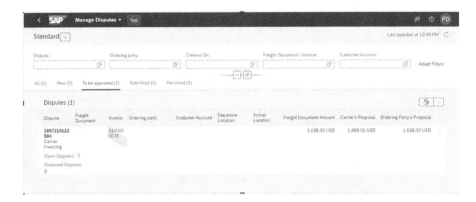

Figure 6-45. *Manage dispute application*

3. The carrier can either accept the proposal from
    the ordering party (TM system) or they can
    propose new charge against it.

Screenshot from SAP LBN Carrier Tenant

Figure 6-46. *Manage dispute application*

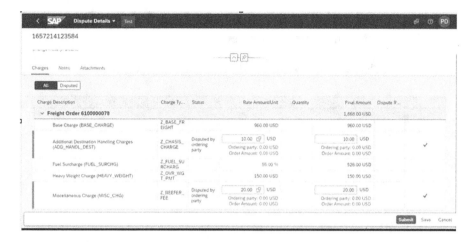

Figure 6-47. *Manage dispute application*

4. To accept the charge against disputed lines, select the green tick appearing in the last column, at the end of the row. Once accepted, the status of that charge type line item would change to "Accepted by carrier."

Screenshot from SAP LBN Carrier Tenant

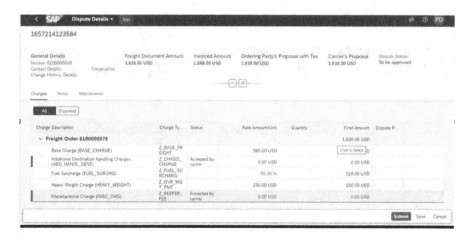

Figure 6-48. *Manage dispute application*

5. Select the "Submit" button at the end of the
    screen to submit the new invoice.

Screenshot from SAP LBN Carrier Tenant

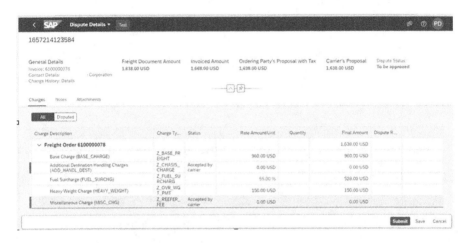

Figure 6-49. *Manage dispute application*

6. The carrier can navigate to the "Manage
    Invoices" Fiori app to resubmit the
    invoice to SAP.

Screenshot from SAP LBN Carrier Tenant

Figure 6-50. *Manage invoice*

7. The carrier would be able to see the invoice under Ready for resubmission status.

Screenshot from SAP LBN Carrier Tenant

Figure 6-51. *Manage invoice*

8. Click the "Submit" button to submit and share the invoice with SAP TM.

Screenshot from SAP LBN Carrier Tenant

Figure 6-52. *Manage invoice*

Figure 6-53. Manage invoice

9. The new invoice is generated in the Freight
    Order Document flow.

Screenshot from SAP TM

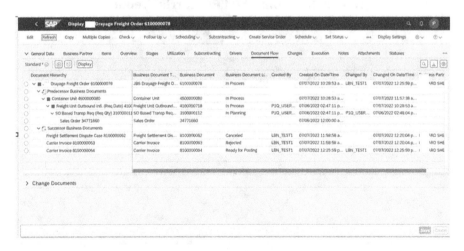

Figure 5-54. Freight order

BN4L (LBN): Events from Carrier Tenant

In the SAP BN4L, the "Events from Carrier Tenant" functionality serves as a critical component in enabling real-time visibility and seamless communication between shippers and carriers. This feature allows carriers operating within their tenant to report significant logistics events directly to the network, ensuring that all stakeholders are kept up-to-date on the progress of freight orders. Through the Carrier Tenant, events such as departure, arrival, delays, proof of delivery, or unforeseen exceptions can be logged and transmitted to the SAP Logistics Business Network (LBN) platform in real time. These events are systematically captured and shared with the shipper, providing a comprehensive overview of the shipment's status and supporting end-to-end supply chain visibility. Additionally, event reporting from the Carrier Tenant integrates seamlessly with the SAP Transportation Management (TM) system, ensuring that every reported event is updated in the freight order and transportation planning. This integration reduces the dependency on manual communication, thereby minimizing errors and delays in information exchange. Furthermore, the flexibility of the "Events from Carrier Tenant" functionality allows for custom event types to be defined and transmitted based on specific business requirements, supporting a tailored approach to logistics operations. By leveraging this feature, shippers benefit from enhanced transparency, reduced risks, and improved decision-making capabilities, all of which contribute to greater efficiency and customer satisfaction. Ultimately, this robust event management mechanism within the Carrier Tenant underscores SAP's commitment to providing innovative solutions for modern, connected supply chain ecosystems.

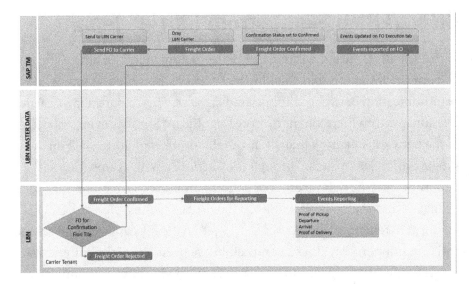

Figure 6-55. *Event processing process flow*

- **Event Types**

    - **Planned Events**: These are predefined milestones
      or checkpoints in the transportation process, such
      as departure, arrival, loading, or unloading. They
      are set up in SAP TM to track the expected progress
      of shipments.

    - **Actual Events**: These are real-time updates
      reported by carriers or other stakeholders,
      reflecting the actual status of the shipment. For
      example, an "Actual Departure" event confirms that
      the shipment has left the origin location.

    - **Unplanned Events**: These are unexpected
      occurrences, such as delays, damages, or route
      deviations. They are critical for identifying and
      addressing exceptions in the transportation
      process.

- **Event Reporting**

  - Carriers and other stakeholders can report events through various channels, such as the SAP Logistics Business Network (LBN) portal, EDI (Electronic Data Interchange), or APIs.

  - These events are transmitted to SAP TM, where they are matched with the corresponding freight orders or shipments.

Figure 6-56. *GTT integration*

Access the activity using one of the following navigation options:

SAP Menu	*Carrier Tenant* ➤ *Freight Orders Management* ➤ *Freight Orders for Reposting*

Workflow Steps

In this scenario, the carrier is already onboarded to LBN.

Prerequisites:

1. Carrier is onboarded to LBN.

2. Carrier has confirmed the FO.

The following events can be posted on FO from Carrier Tenant:

- Arrival

- Departure

- Proof of pickup

- Proof of delivery

Step 1: Freight Orders for Reporting

Access Fiori tile "**Freight Orders for Reporting**" from Carrier Tenant, and select your FO.

Screenshot from SAP LBN Carrier Tenant

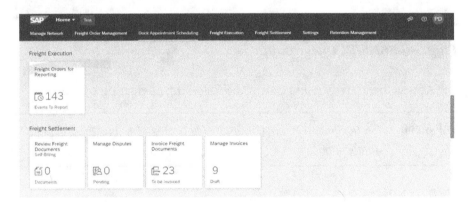

Figure 6-57. *LBN freight order reporting application*

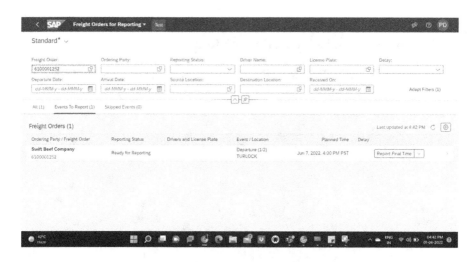

Figure 6-58. *LBN freight order reporting application*

The Freight Orders for Reporting app enables you to keep your ordering parties informed about the transportation of their freight. For example, if one of your delivery trucks is delayed en route, you can send the ordering party a new ETA (expected time of arrival) so they can replan if necessary. Additionally, the app lets you upload and send documents, such as proof of deliveries, to your ordering parties.

There are various reporting statuses (Ready for Reporting, Reporting in Progress, Reporting in Progress (freight order reconfirmation required), Reporting Completed, Canceled). You can use the filter criteria to locate the freight orders which are ready for reporting.

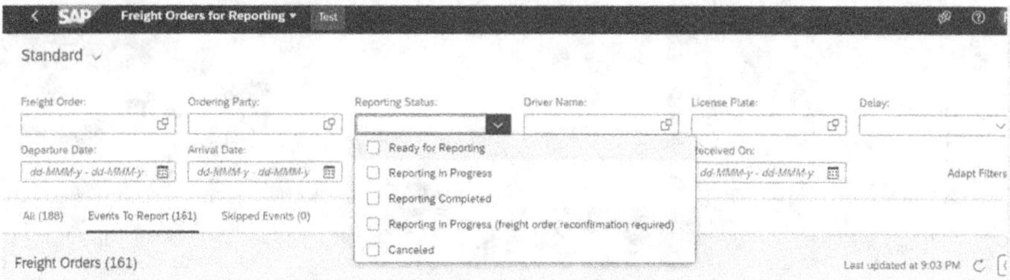

Figure 6-59. *LBN freight order reporting application*

239

After selecting your freight order, navigate to the "**Reporting**" tab.

Screenshot from SAP LBN Carrier Tenant

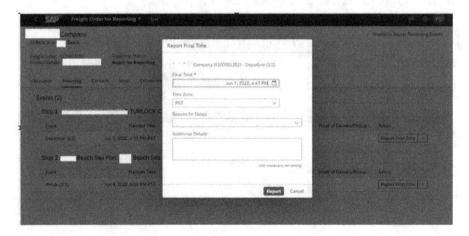

Figure 6-60. *LBN freight order reporting application*

Step 2: Event Reporting

Reporting final times for arrival and departure would post events arrival and departure on FO.

Post Departure Event

Screenshot from SAP LBN Carrier Tenant

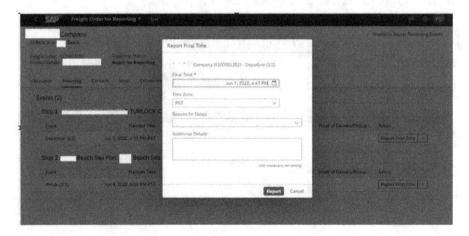

Figure 6-61. *LBN freight order reporting application*

Screenshot from SAP TM

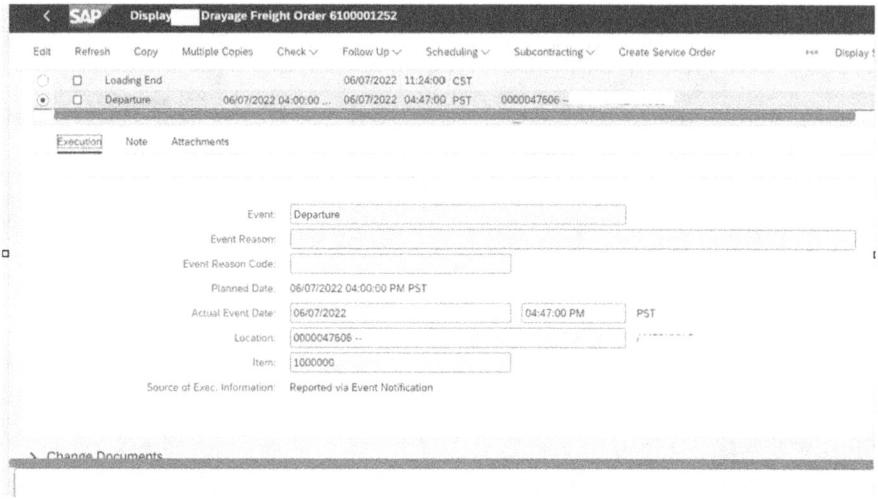

Figure 6-62. *Freight order*

Post Arrival Event

Screenshot from SAP LBN Carrier Tenant

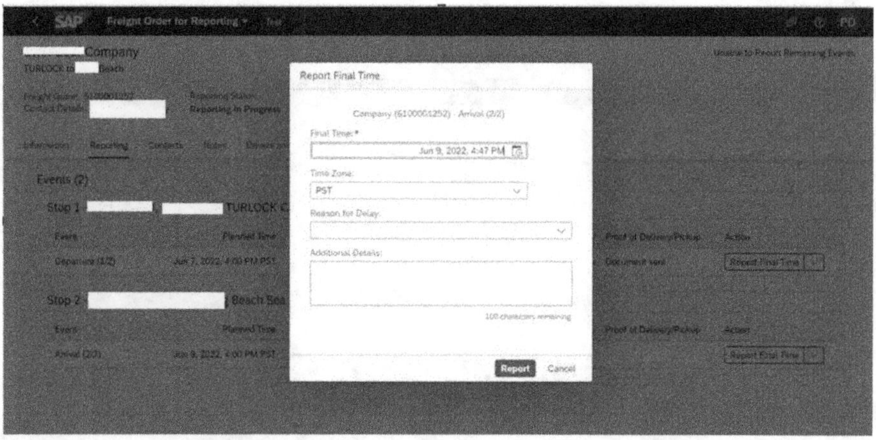

Figure 6-63. *Freight order*

Screenshot from SAP TM

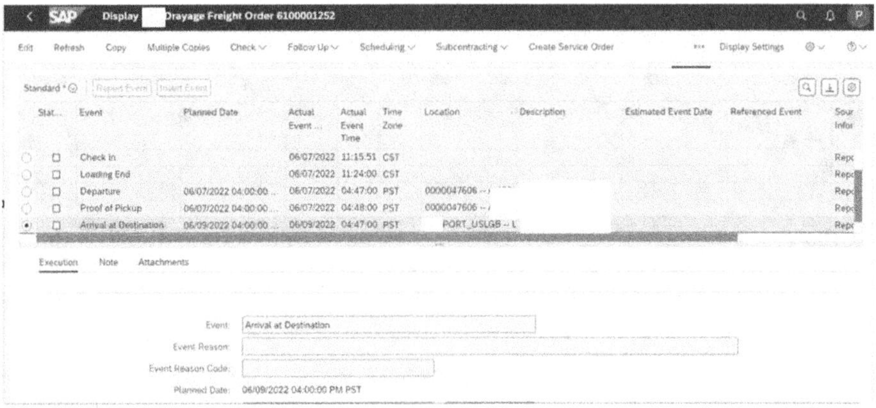

Figure 6-64. *Freight order*

Similarly, carriers can post events Proof of Pickup and Proof of Delivery by selecting the same from the drop-down and adding the **attachment** as proof.

Post Proof of Pickup

The carrier can add proof as attachment by clicking the "Upload" button.

Screenshot from SAP LBN Carrier Tenant

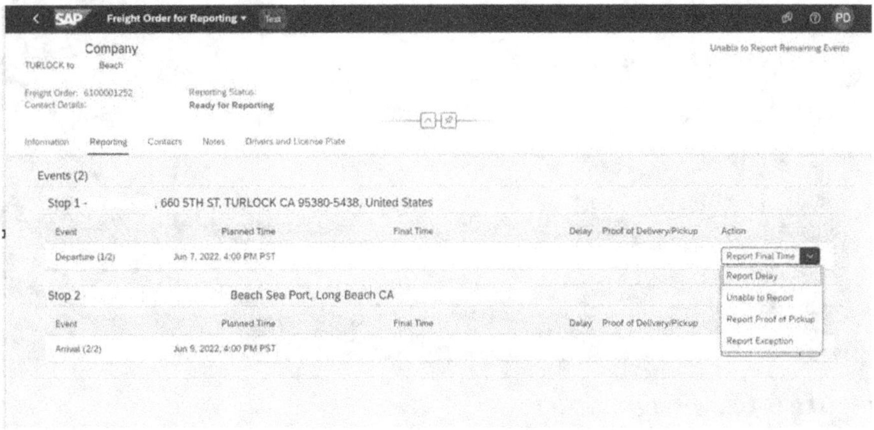

Figure 6-65. *Freight order reporting application*

Figure 6-66. *Freight order reporting application*

Once reported, this event would be visible under the SAP TM
Execution tab SAP TM.

Screenshot from SAP TM

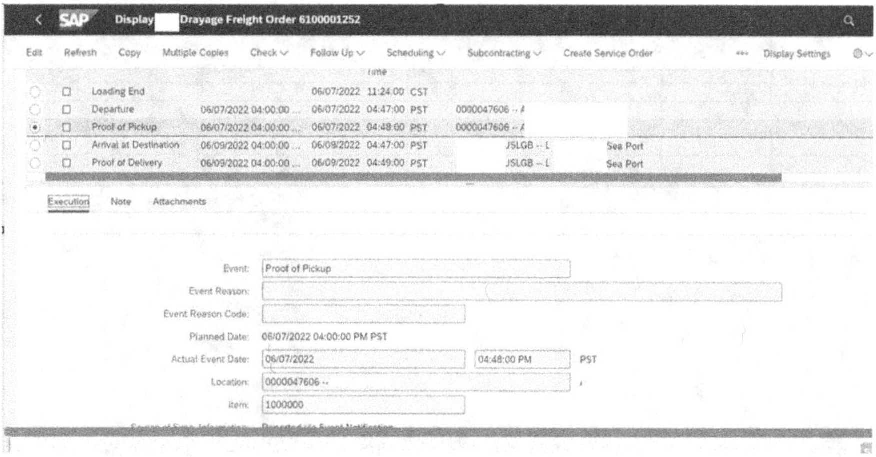

Figure 6-67. *Freight order*

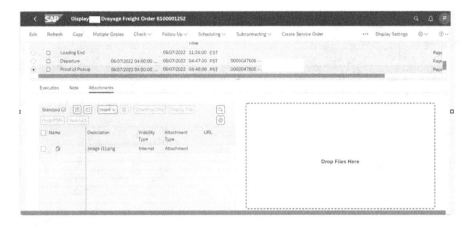

Figure 6-68. *Freight order*

Post Proof of Delivery

The carrier can add proof as attachment by clicking the "Upload" button as seen below.

Screenshot from SAP LBN Carrier Tenant

Figure 6-69. *Freight order reporting application*

And it would reflect under the Execution tab of freight order in SAP TM.

Screenshot from SAP TM

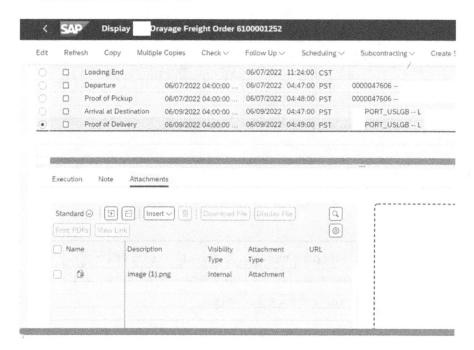

Figure 6-70. Freight order

Invite Business Partners

The Invite Business Partners app is designed for managing all the business partners that you want to be part of your network. You can use this app to select and invite business partners to join your business network and check their participation status. If you have access, you can navigate to the Discover Business Partners app to find more potential business partners.

- **Worklist (Manage Business Partners)**

  - *To Be Submitted*

    The To Be Submitted worklist displays all the business partners that you have uploaded or added in the app but have not yet submitted to the back-end team of SAP Logistics Business Network to manage the connection invitations.

  - *In Progress*

    The In Progress worklist displays all the business partners that you have submitted to the back-end team to manage the connection invitations.

  - *Accepted*

    The Accepted worklist displays all the business partners who have accepted your invitation to join your business network.

  - *Rejected*

    The Rejected worklist displays all the business partners who have rejected your invitation to join your business network via Discover Business Partners.

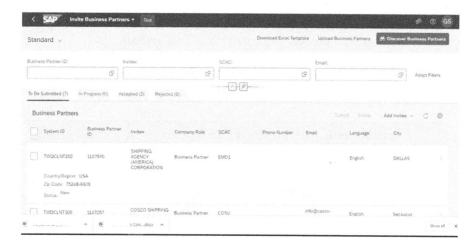

Figure 6-71. *Invite business partner Fiori screen*

- **Add New Business Partners**

  You can add new business partners to the Invite
  Business Partners app in one of the following ways.

  Manual Entry

  On the To Be Submitted tab, you can manually add a
  new business partner to the Invite Business Partners
  app by choosing Add Invitee Business Partner. You
  can also add a shipper to the app by choosing Add
  Invitee Shipper. When adding a shipper, you must
  provide the shipper's LBN ID.

  Manual Entry with an Excel Template

  You can download the Excel template available in
  the Invite Business Partners app by choosing the
  "Download Excel Template" button. You can fill the
  details of the business partners using this template.
  You can then upload this template back in the Invite
  Business Partners app.

Downloading business partner Excel from the SAP
Transportation Management (SAP TM) system.

You can download the list of business partners
in your SAP TM system and upload the Excel file
in the Invite Business Partners app. For more
information, see Download Carrier Excel from the
SAP Transportation Management system.

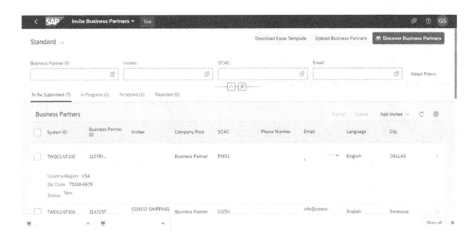

Figure 6-72. *Invite business partner Fiori screen*

- **Connection Invitations**

  Once you have a list of business partners added to the
  Invite Business Partners app, you can select one or
  more partners from the To Be Submitted worklist and
  choose "Submit."

  Once you choose "Submit," the system instantaneously
  sends a request to the back-end team of SAP Logistics
  Business Network to manage the connection invitation.
  The system moves the submitted business partners to
  the In Progress worklist.

Instead of using the "Submit" button in Invite Business
Partners to send connection invitations to business
partners, test shippers and system integration shippers
use the Discover Business Partners app to find business
partners and send invitations to them.

Figure 6-73. *Invite business partner Fiori screen*

Figure 6-74. *Invite business partner Fiori screen*

- **Recall Invitations**

  You can recall a submitted invitation if its status remains "In Progress." To do this, switch to the In Progress worklist, click to open the invitation that you want to recall, and then choose Recall on the details page.

  After being recalled, the invitation returns to the To Be Submitted worklist and becomes editable. The business partner cannot view the recalled invitation using the app until you submit it again.

- **Downloading Business Partner Excel from SAP TM**

  You can download the business partners from the SAP TM system and upload them to the Invite Business Partners app.

  1. Execute the report /SCMTMS/R_LBN_CARR_LIST_DWNLD in transaction SE38.

  2. Enter your SAP TM organization ID in the Organizational ID field and execute.

  3. Alternatively, instead of entering an organization ID and retrieving multiple business partners, you can also enter the business partner IDs in the Carrier IDs field and execute.

  4. Select all the business partners that you want to download, and then, choose Download.

Figure 6-75. *Download Excel*

- **Updating LBN IDs in SAP TM**

  You can update the SAP TM system with the unique
  LBN IDs of the business partners who have accepted
  to connect with your business network.

  1. Download the list of business partners with
      their LBN IDs from the Accepted worklist in the
      Invite Business Partners app.

  2. In the SAP TM system, execute the report
      /SCMTMS/R_LBN_ID_BP_UPD in
      transaction SA38.

  3. Browse for the CSV file that you have
      downloaded, and upload the file.

Summary

This chapter explores the crucial role of transportation management in optimizing logistics operations, with a focus on SAP Transportation Management (SAP TM) and SAP BN4L. These tools enable organizations to manage the movement of goods efficiently, improving visibility, collaboration, and decision-making across the supply chain. The chapter emphasizes the **Freight Order Confirmation by Carrier**, a process that ensures carriers acknowledge and accept freight orders, marking the start of the transportation process and aligning both the shipper and carrier on expectations.

Key points covered in the chapter include

- **Freight Order Confirmation**: This process involves the carrier's acknowledgment of the freight order, confirming the availability of capacity and marking the commencement of transportation activities. SAP TM plays a central role by initiating the order, selecting the carrier, and updating the status upon receiving confirmation.

- **Role of SAP TM**: SAP TM handles the entire freight order life cycle, from creation and carrier selection to the confirmation and execution of the order. The system allows for real-time updates and exception handling to ensure smooth transportation operations.

- **SAP BN4L's Role in Freight Order Confirmation**: SAP BN4L facilitates seamless communication between the shipper and carrier. It ensures the real-time exchange of freight orders, carrier confirmations, and updates, which enhances collaboration and provides better visibility into the status of transportation activities.

- **Dispute and Invoicing in SAP BN4L:** The platform aids in managing invoicing and dispute resolution, ensuring accurate billing and the quick resolution of discrepancies, which is vital for maintaining positive relationships and smooth operations in the logistics network.

- **Events from the Carrier Tenant in SAP BN4L:** This section covers how SAP BN4L handles events originating from the Carrier Tenant, such as shipment departures, arrivals, milestones, and exceptions. These events are critical for real-time tracking, improving communication, and enabling businesses to proactively manage any disruptions in the logistics process.

Overall, the chapter highlights how SAP TM and SAP BN4L work together to streamline logistics operations, improve visibility, and enhance collaboration across the supply chain. By leveraging these technologies, businesses can better manage freight orders, track shipments, and resolve any issues that may arise, ensuring timely deliveries and optimized transportation processes.

CHAPTER 7

Troubleshooting and Integration Logs

In SAP BN4L, **Integration Logs** are essential tools for monitoring and troubleshooting the data exchange between SAP systems and external partners, such as carriers or shippers. These logs provide detailed insights into the communication processes, ensuring that all transactions and events are accurately recorded and any issues are promptly identified and resolved. Here's a breakdown of their key aspects:

1. **Purpose**

   - Integration logs track the flow of data between SAP Transportation Management (TM), SAP Logistics Business Network (LBN), and external systems.

   - They help ensure that messages, such as freight orders, event updates, and invoices, are successfully transmitted and received.

2. **Components**

   - **Message Logs**: These logs capture the details of each message exchanged, including timestamps, sender and receiver information, and message content.

© Prince Tyagi, Anevershika 2025
P. Tyagi and Anevershika, *Getting Started with BN4L and GTT Integrations for SAP*,
https://doi.org/10.1007/979-8-8688-1405-1_7

- **Error Logs**: If a message fails to transmit or encounters an issue, the error logs provide detailed information about the problem, such as missing data or connectivity issues.

- **Status Logs**: These logs indicate the current status of messages, such as "Sent," "Received," "Processed," or "Failed."

3. **Accessing Integration Logs**

- Integration logs can be accessed through the SAP LBN portal or the SAP TM interface, depending on the configuration.

- Administrators and users with appropriate permissions can view and analyze the logs to ensure smooth operations.

4. **Troubleshooting**

- When an issue is identified, the logs provide detailed error messages and diagnostic information to help resolve the problem.

- Common issues include data mismatches, connectivity errors, or delays in message processing.

In SAP Global Track and Trace (GTT), the **View Log Tiles** are essential tools designed to provide administrators with a comprehensive overview of message processing, event handling, and integration activities. These tiles are part of the GTT interface and are instrumental in ensuring the reliability and transparency of supply chain operations. Here's how they function:

1. **Message Logs**

   - The **Message Log Tile** offers a snapshot of the status of messages exchanged between systems, such as "Processed," "Failed," or "Pending."

   - Administrators can drill down into specific messages to view details like timestamps, payloads, and process flows.

   - This tile also allows for manual retriggering of failed messages, ensuring quick resolution of issues.

2. **Event Logs**

   - The **Event Log Tile** provides insights into the status of events, such as planned and actual milestones or exceptions.

   - It categorizes events by their processing status or error codes, enabling administrators to identify and address issues efficiently.

   - Detailed event histories and payloads can be accessed for troubleshooting and analysis.

3. **Integration Logs**

   - The **Integration Log Tile** aggregates logs related to inbound and outbound messages between SAP GTT, back-end systems (like SAP S/4HANA), and external partners.

   - It highlights failed or escalated messages, allowing administrators to reprocess them and resolve issues like missing configurations or service unavailability.

4. **Visualization and Navigation**

- Each tile uses visual elements, such as charts or graphs, to provide a quick overview of the system's health and performance.

- Clicking on a specific section of a chart navigates users to detailed views, such as the "Manage Message View" or "Event Details" page.

5. **Proactive Issue Resolution**

- The tiles enable proactive monitoring by providing real-time updates and alerts for critical issues.

- Administrators can configure rules for automatic retriggering of events or messages, enhancing system reliability.

Process Flow

Below are process flow outlines the sequential steps involved in managing transportation orders and related business processes. It typically begins with the creation or receipt of a transportation order, followed by the generation of quotations and notifications. These orders are then processed through SAP Transportation Management, where charge management and batch processing are handled to ensure accuracy and efficiency. Freight orders are managed and monitored throughout the process, with any disputes or exceptions addressed as needed, particularly in scenarios involving Stock Transport Orders (STO) and Sales Orders (SO). This structured flow ensures seamless coordination between warehousing, transportation, and distribution activities, supporting both domestic and international logistics operation.

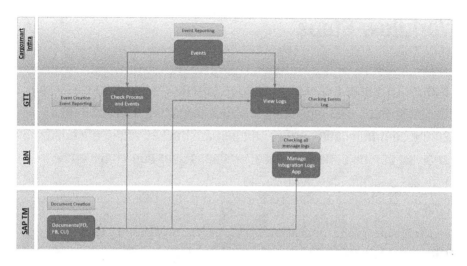

Figure 7-1. *Integration process flow*

Procedure

Access the activity using one of the following navigation options:

SAP Menu	*Shipper Tenant* ➤ *Business Operations* ➤ *Manage Integration Logs*
Transaction Code	SRT_MONI
Selection Screen	

Workflow Steps

Note   This user manual is intended for informative purpose to see the integration messages failures/successes within LBN tenants so the communication errors can be backtracked and root cause analysis can be done with ease. Business user don't have any process specific steps to execute.

Step 1: Monitoring Integration Message in LBN Global Track and Trace Tenant

View Logs App

This app allows you to have an at-a-glance overview of the available logs and their statuses, based on the data from the following sub-views:

  a.   Manage Message Logs (MML)

  b.   Manage Event Logs (MEL)

  c.   Manage Integration Logs (MIL)

  1.   Go to "View Logs" app in GTT

   Screenshot from SAP GTT

Figure 7-2. *Integration log*

2. Each of the three views are described in detail below.

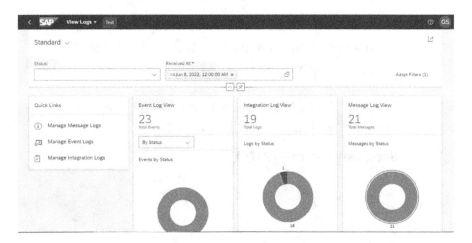

Figure 7-3. *Integration log*

a. **Manage Event Logs View**

This app allows assigned users to view all the
technical logs for all the event data, phase by phase,
and, if necessary, retrigger one or multiple events or
their correlations.

The tasks associated with this app include the
following:

- Displays a list of all the events (tracked process
  events and actual events) and their correlations

- Displays log details for each event including its
  process flow, process history, and payload

- Displays log details for each correlation about its
  process history, phase by phase

- Enables historical events and correlations, within a
  retention period (which is configured in the MML
  app), to be retriggered

Click "Event Log View," and set the filters for received
date/time and status as required.

Screenshot from SAP GTT

Figure 7-4. *Integration log*

Find the message by looking up for the relevant tracking
ID, and check details of message. If message got failed,
you can retrigger the message.

Screenshot from SAP GTT

Figure 7-5. *Integration log*

b. **Manage Integration Logs View**

With this app, you can monitor the inbound and outbound integration messages related to location replication and visibility providers that are processed by SAP Logistics Business Network.

In this view, you can use the following worklists:

- **Failed**: The system assigns this status to a message when there is a syntax error that occurred during the processing of an iFlow or when there is a payload issue such as missing mandatory field or a missing configuration.

- **Retry**: The system assigns this status to a message when the service is not available for a short period. During this time, the system periodically retires to process the message. When the system is unable to process till the end of this time, it moves the message into escalated status.

- **Escalated**: The system assigns this status to a message when the service is not available for a longer period or when there is a payload issue such as missing mandatory field or a missing configuration.

- **Completed**: The system assigns this status to a message when the iFlows were able to process the document successfully.

- **Submitted for Reprocessing**: The system assigns this status to a message when you reprocess a message. After you solve the configuration or syntax issues in SAP Logistics Business Network, and when you select the Reprocess button, the system moves the message to this status. The system revaluates the status of the entries in this tab, and based on the feedback from SAP Cloud Integration, the messages may or may not move to other statuses.

c. **Manage Message Logs View**

This app allows assigned users to view all the technical logs for all the message data, phase by phase, and, if necessary, retrigger certain events or their correlations for the message.

The tasks associated with this app include the following:

- Displays a list of all the messages used to update a process or for business actual event reporting

- Displays log details for each message including its process flow and payload

- Displays log details for each event including its process history and payload

- Displays log details for each correlation about its process history, phase by phase

- Enables historical events and correlations, within a retention period, to be retriggered.

Note   This app is shared with Freight Collaboration tenant of LBN as well.

Detailed view of the message received in GTT tenant

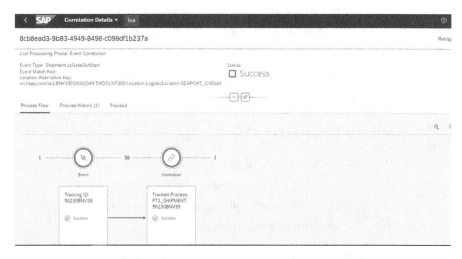

Figure 7-6. *Integration log*

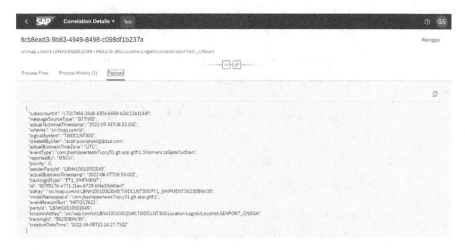

Figure 7-7. *Integration log*

Step 2: Monitoring Integration Message in LBN Freight Collaboration Tenant

Manage Integration Logs App

Shippers and carriers can monitor the inbound and outbound messages that are processed from SAP Logistics Business Network, Freight Collaboration option.

With this app, data contributors can view all integration logs for solution owner and data contributor transactions in SAP Logistics Business Network, Global Track and Trace option.

When you launch the app, the system displays the main view with the following areas:

Filter Bar: Using the filter bar in the header, you can filter the integration logs to restrict the number of logs displayed. You can filter based on one or more of the log details such as document ID, from time, to time, and correlation ID.

Worklists: You can use the following worklists: Failed, Escalated, Retry, Submitted for Reprocessing, and Completed.

1.   Go to Manage Integration Logs App in LBN.

Screenshot from SAP Shipper Tenant

Figure 7-8. *Integration log*

2. Worklist view:

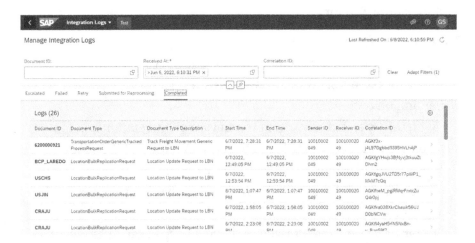

Figure 7-9. *Integration log*

3. You can see error details in the message log.

Screenshot from SAP Shipper Tenant

Figure 7-10. *Integration log*

Summary

The integration of **SAP BN4L** Freight Collaboration and **SAP Global Track and Trace (SAP GTT)** brings together the power of collaborative logistics with end-to-end visibility and control over supply chain processes. By combining the advanced functionalities of these two SAP solutions, businesses can achieve a more transparent, efficient, and agile logistics operation.

SAP BN4L is a cloud-based platform that facilitates real-time collaboration between all stakeholders in the logistics ecosystem, including suppliers, logistics providers, carriers, and shippers. It allows businesses to streamline their logistics workflows, improve communication, and optimize processes such as freight management, shipment tracking, and invoicing.

SAP GTT is a solution that provides real-time tracking and monitoring capabilities for goods across the entire supply chain, from origin to destination. It captures event-based data such as shipment status, milestones, and exceptions, offering unparalleled visibility into the transportation process. By using **SAP GTT**, organizations can track shipments, detect potential delays, and manage exceptions in real time, helping to optimize the flow of goods and improve decision-making.

Integration Log

The **integration log** serves as a crucial tool for tracking the data flow between **SAP BN4L** and **SAP GTT**. It logs all integration activities, providing a transparent view of the data exchange process between the two systems. This log is essential for

- **Monitoring Data Transfer**: The integration log captures all data transfers between **SAP BN4L** and **SAP GTT**, ensuring that the integration process is running smoothly and data is being exchanged correctly. This log allows businesses to monitor the flow of event-based information and verify that it has been successfully received and processed.

269

- **Troubleshooting Issues**: If there are any discrepancies or issues with the integration, the log can help identify the root cause. It allows system administrators or IT teams to troubleshoot any errors that might occur in the data synchronization process, ensuring that the integration runs without interruption.

- **Audit and Compliance**: The integration log maintains an audit trail of all transactions and events, providing transparency into the data exchange. This audit trail is crucial for compliance purposes, as it ensures that all actions taken in the system are properly documented and verifiable.

The integration of **SAP BN4L** Freight Collaboration and **SAP GTT** is a game-changer for businesses looking to optimize their logistics and supply chain management processes. By providing real-time event tracking, enhanced collaboration, and end-to-end visibility, this integration helps organizations make informed decisions, improve customer satisfaction, and reduce supply chain disruptions. The integration log further ensures transparency, accountability, and efficient troubleshooting, making it an essential tool for managing the flow of data between these two powerful SAP solutions.

Index

© Prince Tyagi, Anevershika 2025
P. Tyagi and Anevershika, *Getting Started with BN4L and GTT Integrations for SAP*,
https://doi.org/10.1007/979-8-8688-1405-1

L

M, N

S

www.ingramcontent.com/pod-product-compliance
Lightning Source LLC
LaVergne TN
LVHW051637050326
832903LV00022B/792

*9 7 9 8 8 6 8 8 1 4 0 4 4 *